Tackling Rugby

Tackling Rugby

What Every Parent Should Know About Injuries

Allyson M. Pollock

VERSO
London • New York

First published by Verso 2014
© Allyson M. Pollock 2014

1 3 5 7 9 10 8 6 4 2

Verso
UK: 6 Meard Street, London W1F 0EG
US: 20 Jay Street, Suite 1010, Brooklyn, NY 11201
www.versobooks.com

Verso is the imprint of New Left Books

ISBN-13: 978-1-78168-602-7
eISBN-13: 978-1-78168-671-3 (UK)
eISBN-13: 978-1-78168-603-4 (US)

British Library Cataloguing in Publication Data
A catalogue record for this book is available from the British Library

Library of Congress Cataloging-in-Publication Data
A catalog record for this book is available from the Library of Congress

Typeset in Fournier by MJ & N Gavan, Truro, Cornwall
Printed and bound by CPI Group (UK) Ltd, Croydon, CR0 4YY

For Hamish and Hector and their cousins,
Lucy, Patrick, Olivia, Alastair, Neil, Kelly,
Jamie, Catriona, Rory, Rebecca, Annie,
and for all children who love to play

For Ian Basnett

Contents

Introduction

Play the Ball, Not the Child

Today in the United Kingdom it is almost impossible to have a rational conversation about the risks of rugby to children without provoking shrill cries about the 'nanny state'. Every year more names are added to the list of children seriously, and occasionally fatally, injured playing the game, yet our schools, sporting authorities and government departments are failing even to properly monitor rugby injuries or assess the risks. It is as if we have collectively chosen the bliss that comes with wilful ignorance to avoid the uncomfortable truth that the evidence may reveal.

Throughout the playing season, images of heads slamming against heads, bodies colliding with bodies are beamed to our TV screens from the grand stadia of the professional game. The same is happening on the windswept school pitches where our children compete. For every man injured in professional play, thousands of young boys and girls are being hurt. The vast majority of them will never make professional players, but no matter. Believing that the game is their moment of glory, the children throw themselves into the fray until, damaged, they are discarded, and new children take their place.

Studies show that injuries to children as a result of rugby are common, and can have very serious consequences. We need to have an urgent debate about whether the rules of children's rugby should be radically changed, and whether it should remain a compulsory sport in some schools. This book does not call for an outright ban on school rugby, but it does demand that more rigorous evidence is collected to inform a discussion about how this much-loved game can be made safe for children. Once the true facts about rugby injuries become widely known, many parents may indeed be moved to call for a ban on school rugby. But as a matter of urgency we must, at the very least, ask why parents are not required to give consent for their children to play; why rugby remains a compulsory part of the curriculum in many schools; and why we do not systematically monitor and publicise the risk of injury from what is obviously a dangerous sport.

Original research presented in these pages suggests that children playing rugby have at least a one-in-six chance of being seriously injured during a season. A separate study, from an accident and emergency department in Northern Ireland, found that 43 per cent of all sport-related injuries in secondary school children were attributed to rugby, three times more than any other sport.[1] Evidence confirms that injuries resulting in a prolonged absence from rugby and from school are common, and often bring wider physical, financial and psychological costs for children and their parents.[2] A significant proportion of injured children do not return to play within three weeks, and their injuries can have a profound impact on confidence and education. There is an established, although small, risk of permanent disability and even death from playing rugby.[3] Crucially, a large proportion of young players who have suffered serious injury believe that it was preventable.[4]

Concerns about the safety of rugby, especially for young players, are not new. For over thirty years there have been warnings.[5] The evidence is stacking up, despite this being a shockingly neglected area of study. But the issue has been obscured and hidden from public gaze; injuries are 'rugby's dirty secret'.[6]

In January 2011, fourteen-year-old Benjamin Peter Robinson from Northern Ireland collapsed on the rugby field after a tackle in the final minutes of a match. He later died. At his inquest in September 2013, the coroner ruled that Benjamin died from 'second-impact syndrome'. Second-impact (or double-impact) syndrome occurs when a player sustains a second brain trauma before recovering fully from a prior concussion or other serious brain injury. Benjamin had continued to play for twenty-five minutes following two heavy collisions and concussion, before a final blow killed him.[7] Criticism was levelled at the school for allegedly attempting to hush the matter up, and the police initially failed to investigate properly. It was the children who finally spoke out, saying they knew that Benjamin had been knocked out earlier in the game and that he 'didn't look right'.[8]

Lucas Neville is another victim of the game, although he has lived to tell the tale. He was just eighteen years old, a brilliant scholar and in the last year of school, when called upon to play in the last minutes of a school match, despite having previously been concussed in rugby training. He suffered a second, serious brain injury that left him seriously and permanently disabled. He is now suing the school and the hospital in Dublin for more than €5 million in damages for negligence – the school for failing in its duty of care to him.[9]

Although, shamefully, the cases of Benjamin Robinson and Lucas Neville received very little attention from politicians at the time, they did highlight just how high the stakes are. Several of the injuries commonly sustained by rugby-playing children are extremely serious. Concussion is one of them. Aside from the risk of second-impact syndrome, head injury can cause internal haemorrhaging and bleeding, hearing loss, blindness and long-term or permanent damage to the brain. Then there are the spinal injuries also prevalent in the game, especially among forwards, which can leave young players paralysed for life. A glance at the websites of charities like Hearts and Balls, set up to help seriously injured players, reveals the hidden dark side of rugby and the anguish of so many families struggling to cope with the life-long consequences of a single moment on the pitch. And not to be underestimated, there are the smashed bones and torn ligaments that can cause lasting physical damage, put an end to the enjoyment of sport and have profound psychological effects. Most of these injuries occur during tackles and scrums – the contact elements of the sport.

One thing is for sure, we are not doing enough to prevent these injuries, and that will only change when the tyranny of silence surrounding the subject is broken. If the arguments for changes to the game or a ban on children's rugby sound extreme in the current climate, it is only because our ignorance is so deep and the taboo of speaking out so great. Information on school rugby injury is scanty because rugby unions and public authorities have conveniently failed to collect systematic data or to provide parents with clear information about known risks. The refusal to make a serious attempt to gather that evidence raises the question of why so little is being done.

A key explanation is the commercial power of the sport itself. That power, concentrated in the top-tiers of the professional rugby unions, recoils at the idea of proper monitoring of rugby injuries, perhaps because it knows that the facts could create a backlash of bad publicity and litigation and put parents and children off the game.

Rugby unions are large businesses. Over an eight-year period (2004/5 to 2012/13) the English Rugby Football Union (RFU) grew its revenue by 81 per cent, from £84.8 million[10] to £153.5 million[11] – by far the biggest revenue of any rugby union in the world. During the same period, the revenue of the Welsh Rugby Union grew by 48 per cent to £61 million,[12] and its Irish counterpart grew its revenue by 58 per cent to €61.2 million.[13] Rugby union as a whole was the fastest growing market of any sport globally from 2005 to 2009.[14] A look through the accounts of these unions reveals a preoccupation with income generation – recruiting players, growing the fan base and expanding corporate and government sponsorship.

In England, viewing figures for international rugby demonstrate the game's popularity. In 2011, the Six Nations tournament matches attracted an average of 4.6 million viewers, with the most-watched match, between England and France, being seen by 9.6 million people on BBC1.[15]

In terms of participation, rugby union is the most popular high-impact collision sport and the third most popular team contact sport worldwide.[16] There are an estimated 6.6 million rugby union players in the world, across 119 countries; 2.4 million of them are registered players and around 1.5 million are women players.[17] The sport is increasing in popularity internationally, with a hundred countries now occupying a world ranking, and rugby union 'sevens' (an abbreviated form of the game) returning to the Olympic Games in 2016. However, compared to the big international sports the numbers involved are still small – football had 38.3 million registered players worldwide in 2005.[18]

The rugby unions need parents to send their boys and girls into the system, from school teams to junior clubs to college and university teams. Without them there can be no game. As the *Guardian* reported of the English RFU, 'Among various initiatives is a desire to install Wi-Fi into more rugby clubhouses, on the basis that modern teenagers won't hang around long there otherwise. A World Cup on home soil in 2015 is also a perfect opportunity to encourage more women to embrace the sport, both on and off the field. In terms of inspiring the next generation it promises to be English rugby's Olympic moment.'[19]

England has the largest number of rugby union players of any country in the world. It is estimated that 1.2 million children play rugby in schools and clubs in England. However, between April 2012 and April 2013, only 0.5 per cent of the over-sixteen population of England played rugby union or league regularly, compared to 6.6 per cent who went swimming, 4.5 per cent who took part in athletics and 4.5 per cent who played football.[20] So in England and parts of Scotland, rugby union is widening its base from its roots as an elite sport for public school boys. In the last few years, in an effort to expand its income, rugby has extended its reach, opening its doors to both genders, as well as all ages and social classes. Rugby unions are targeting new initiatives at poorer areas, such as Newham in East London and parts of Lothian in Scotland, to get fresh blood into the game, a drive that will only exacerbate the existing inequalities that see poor children suffer a much higher injury rate than the well-off.[21] More women are taking up the game than ever.[22]

If the numbers playing rugby at youth and amateur levels were to decrease, so too would rugby's support base and, consequently, the sponsorship and broadcast revenue that generates the income for the business. Information about levels of injury is a threat to this business model, which is why requests for data may be met with hostility or refusal. But as I show in Part I, rugby authorities occupy a key role in a web of powerful interests embracing the sport – a web that knits together sport, finance, big business and government. This alliance is a formidable barrier to change.

Of course there are arguments extoling the benefits of rugby. One of the most widely accepted of these is that participation in sport encourages a healthy lifestyle and prevents obesity. It is true that keeping children active and fit is beneficial both for them and for society. The 2009 national survey for England indicated that about 30 per cent of children between the ages of two and fifteen are overweight, while about 14 to 20 per cent are obese.[23]

These rates are the highest in Europe. Obesity reduces life expectancy by an average of three years, or eight to ten years in the case of severe obesity, and costs the NHS around £4 billion annually.[24] The health benefits of sport go well beyond obesity and physical fitness; it can even have a positive effect on mental health.[25]

The impact of rugby on obesity, mental health and physical well-being is not known. Moreover, the advantages of sport do not mean that children should play one that is dangerous. Injured children are not active, and a painful experience can turn a child off sport – many children who give up rugby altogether cite injury as the reason. Evidence shows that participation in sport does not have to equate to injury, but Britain lags badly behind in protecting children from harm. Swedish children have among the highest levels of sports participation in Europe, but the lowest rates of injury and obesity. That has not come about by chance, but due to the range of sports on offer, a well-established injury surveillance system and a determined twenty-year effort to halve childhood injury deaths.[26]

A second common argument for rugby, one that does address the contact element of the sport, is that it acts as a channel for aggression and instills discipline, manliness and courage. From this angle, when parents question the safety of the game they are accused of being overprotective, 'failing to let their children go', 'mollycoddling' or 'wrapping their children up in cotton wool'. For the government, rugby is a form of 'bread and circuses', a means of diffusing male aggression and providing a controlled outlet for the masses. But could it be the other way around – is rugby fuelling aggression? Rugby is a collision sport first and foremost; the violence is not ancillary. The game is designed to allow the kind of high-impact collision that can result in concussion, shattered teeth, smashed cheek-bones and broken spines. Ask any young player and they will say the excitement and fear of physical contact are a heady and petrifying mix.

The same arguments are often had around child boxing. But with that sport, unlike with rugby, there is official, medically led opposition. For nearly three decades, the British Medical Association (BMA) has actively campaigned against children boxing.[27] In 1999, it issued thousands of leaflets for councils to pass to schools and sports clubs warning of the dangers of sustaining brain injury. The BMA called for local authorities to ban boxing on council-owned premises (a third of local authorities give financial support to boxing). As the BMA explained, 'Children think they are immortal and don't really consider the risks of something like boxing, especially when it is long-term, cumulative brain damage.... We don't believe that children can make an informed decision about the dangers of boxing.... Boxing is a totally unsuitable activity for children.'[28] The BMA could say the same about rugby, but it has so far been silent. If it did speak out it would likely be met with a similar response to that which it got from the former boxer Henry Cooper, who said that boxing keeps children off street corners and gives them something to do: 'Boxing has some great benefits but you can't tell those do-gooders at the BMA that.... Where will it all end? You will end up with kids growing up wrapped up in cotton wool.'[29] If the BMA was willing to stand up to these specious arguments over boxing, will it now do the same over rugby?

A supposedly more cerebral defence of rugby comes from libertarians who argue that a ban on children playing the sport would be a limit on their freedoms. This line of attack can be and usually is mounted against virtually all public health initiatives (on smoking, alcohol and diet, for example), accompanied by invective about the nanny state. But in a society, our choices are unavoidably bounded. One person's liberty and freedom can infringe on another's rights and life. Public health advocacy puts the public's right to health first. It is remarkable how often libertarian arguments are put forward not by principled political philosophers or convinced anarchists, but by commercial entities that stand to lose financially from a particular measure.

Instead of the libertarian worldview we should be operating on the precautionary principle. According to this principle, if something carries a suspected risk of harm then it is for its proponents to show that it is *not* harmful. Or, to put it another way, it is better to be safe than sorry. This principle is a guiding doctrine in many areas of law, not least at the level of the European Union where it is particularly associated with environmental policy.[30] The principle implies there is a social responsibility to protect our children from exposure to harm when scientific investigation has found a plausible risk. These protections can be relaxed only if further scientific findings provide sound evidence that no harm will result. But we already know that rugby is a major cause of injury, that far from relaxing the rules we should be tightening them further for children, changing the game completely and allowing it to evolve to a safer form of play.

If rugby were a new medical drug it would be withheld until its efficacy and safety had been proven. We would not want our children to be given medicine to improve their mental or physical health if there was little knowledge of its risks and no attempt had been made to collect data on it. Why should rugby, with its harmful side effects, be any different? Most new drugs are produced for profit. Given the scandals that have engulfed the pharmaceutical industry in recent years, we distrust its motives and expect our public authorities to protect us from exploitation and harm, so we empower them to regulate it. Like the pharmaceutical industry, the professional game of rugby union, which the playing public looks to for rule changes and safety initiatives, is also run for profit and receives large amounts of taxpayer subsidies.[31] It is known that rugby has become increasingly dangerous since it became a professional sport in 1995.[32] So why is it not better regulated?

The law can be used to protect people, and when those people are children we are on particularly strong ground because children have well-defined legal rights. Of course all individuals, irrespective of age, have basic human rights.[33] But the law recognises that children are particularly vulnerable and in need of special protection, and authorities have a special duty of care towards them. This principle is reflected in international as well as national law, and there are legal instruments that can be applied to the question of children's rugby.[34] Chief among these is the 1989 United Nations Convention on the Rights of the Child. The Convention recognises the 'right of the child to rest and leisure, to engage in play and recreational activities appropriate to the age of the child'.[35] Children cannot play sport unless they are fit, and the Convention affirms that children have the 'right to be protected from being hurt and mistreated, physically or mentally'.[36] It places the onus on the government to take all available measures to ensure that children's rights are respected, protected and fulfilled. This implies that the government must provide avenues for children to enjoy their right to play sport, while at the same time doing what it can to prevent children from being exposed to harm or injury.

If children have the right to be protected from harm, the question arises of whether a child can consent to the risk of playing rugby when they may not fully comprehend that risk. Is it the duty of adults to act on the child's right to protection, irrespective of whether the child has consented? And which adults should act? The Convention establishes that it is parents' responsibility to always consider what is best for each child.[37] This must, of course, include the decision on whether to play rugby. It also asserts that rights issues should be handled 'in a manner consistent with the evolving capacities of the child', meaning parents must judge whether rugby is appropriate to their child's physical, mental and even emotional capacities.[38] In other words, it can be argued that parents should have to give consent for their child to play rugby, taking into account the child's development and right to be protected from harm. This is a far cry from the situation at many schools throughout the United Kingdom where rugby is compulsory.

For parents to effectively execute this responsibility they need information and knowledge on the risks of the game. This puts an obligation on governments and public agencies to collect and present sports injury statistics. Helpfully, the

Convention 'does place on governments the responsibility to protect and assist families in fulfilling their essential role as nurturers of children'.[39] Children, too, have 'the right to get information that is important to their health and well-being'.[40]

These provisions do have force in the UK – the UN Convention on the Rights of the Child was ratified by parliament in 1991. They are there to be used by parents or others, if not in court then in exchanges with obstinate schools and in public campaigning. Ideally government and public bodies would be on the side of parents, acting in accordance with the Convention. At the minimum they should collect injury data to inform parents of the risks. But instead, local authorities, health authorities and government are pushing enormous sums of money into supporting and expanding the game of rugby while neglecting injury monitoring to the detriment of children and the game.

In the US, in the case of American football – a contact sport which is also blighted by injuries – it is not parents that are leading the way but the professional players. In the last few years some 4,500 former players joined lawsuits against their league, the NFL, for concealing the dangers of concussion injuries, and in 2013 the league agreed to a huge out-of-court settlement of $765 million.[41] This follows several depression-related suicides, including that of Chicago Bears player Dave Duerson who left a suicide note asking that doctors examine his brain after a life wrecked by concussion.[42] College American football players have also filed suit. Joseph Siprut, a lawyer representing players and their families in legal action over the long-term effects of head injuries, said: 'The idea that five years ago I would

have forbidden my kids to play [American] football is hard
to imagine. It never would have occurred to me. Now,
given what I know about the concussion issue – first as a
lawyer who has litigation, but also as someone who reads
the papers – for me as a parent, I don't think I would ever
let my kids set foot on a football field. Ever.'[43]

Similar legal action has been seen in Canada against the
NHL, the premier ice hockey league for both the US and
its northern neighbour. In May 2013, the family of Derek
Boogaard filed a lawsuit blaming the NHL for brain damage
to their son and for his addiction to prescription painkillers.
Boogaard died in 2011 at the age of twenty-eight, and was
posthumously diagnosed with chronic traumatic encephalopathy, a degenerative brain ailment that can be caused by
repeated blows to the head. The family's lawyers argued
that, 'the NHL drafted Derek Boogaard because it wanted
his massive body to fight in order to enhance ratings, earnings and exposure.'[44]

These kinds of lawsuits could eventually bankrupt professional contact sports in the US and Canada. The title
of a *Chicago Tribune* editorial from April 2013, 'American
football industry is on its deathbed', gives a flavour of the
gravity of the situation.[45] If these professional sports do
go under, it is likely that schools would soon cease to play
them. The same could happen in the UK, although so far
there are no legal precedents and when schools are sued
they often settle out of court, meaning the details of the
cases remain outside the public domain.

Do parents have to wait for professional rugby players
who have been crippled by injury and ill health to lead the
charge, or will they take it upon themselves to protect their

children from harm? To watch parents cheering at rugby matches, preparing the post-game teas, and then when misfortune strikes consoling each other with the idea that a child's injury was 'just bad luck' or 'an accident, just a part of the game', makes you wonder if they ever will. Perhaps there is a deeper cultural explanation for why we continue to let our children play a dangerous sport.[46]

Perhaps it says something about us and our society. Men and women who would recoil in disgust at the sight of a street brawl or close their eyes with horror at the scene of a car crash have no such qualms when they watch rugby players being savaged on the pitch. The state allows one form of violence and not the other, and we and our children are conditioned to accept it. Society makes us conform instead of defending our children from harm. This is how structural and institutional violence works. We watch our children play from the sidelines with crossed fingers hoping that a serious injury won't happen to them and, after an adrenalin-filled moment, breathe a sigh of relief when it is someone else's child who is hurt.

At present, a call to ban rugby for children is so far off the map of public debate that for many it is inconceivable. When not met with anger, such a call is treated with derision, as something that could never happen, that is ridiculous and impossible. But we routinely use the law to protect children, as with the minimum age for buying alcohol, smoking or driving on the roads. In a few years' time, a ban on children playing rugby and other dangerous collision sports may seem just as uncontroversial. Action can take different forms: the rules can be radically changed to minimise the risks of injury so that the game is no longer a contact sport. Most injuries occur as a result of contact, so abolishing the contact part of the game would change it irrevocably; it would not be the same sport, even were it to keep the name. But games do evolve, change or even disappear over time as they are shaped by societal and other pressures.

Radical rule changes to games do not happen overnight. Neither do bans. Take other public health measures. The ban on smoking in public places took almost sixty years to enact, from the famous Doll and Hill study in 1950, which showed the risks of lung cancer were more than twenty-five times greater in smokers than non-smokers, to the legislation in 2005 and 2006 in Scotland and England respectively.[42] The tobacco lobby devoted billions of pounds and mobilised all of its networks of power to distort the debate and pollute the science, helped in the UK by politicians like Kenneth Clarke, the Conservative former health secretary. Clarke was deputy chairman and a director of British American Tobacco from 1998–2007 and argued strongly against anti-smoking measures.[47] It should be noted that the UK lagged behind the US, Canada, New Zealand, Ireland and other countries in bringing in the law. But ultimately the weight of knowledge and research, the efforts of pressure groups like ASH (Action on Smoking and Health), the examples of large class action lawsuits in the US, and a fear of litigation on the part of employers and public authorities proved a powerful combination.[48] On the day the ban came into force there was no public protest, no need for law enforcement. It was a popular and accepted measure. Tobacco sales have fallen and so too have smoking-related illnesses and the burden on the NHS budget.[49]

It is a similar story with alcohol. A ban on alcohol advertising has not been enforced in full and so far the drinks industry's well-resourced opposition to minimum alcohol pricing has been successful.[50] Corporations spend hundreds of millions on advertising, lobbying and constructing a counter-critique for the mainstream media, while also muddying the science. The scale of the resources available is hinted at by the nearly £800 million the industry spends every year promoting alcohol in the UK.[51] Its lobbying reach is extensive – BBC1's *Panorama* programme revealed in 2011 that seven out of sixteen members on the Government and Partners Alcohol Working Group – ostensibly formed to cut excessive drinking and reduce harm – were from the alcohol industry.[52] Don Shenker, chief executive of the charity Alcohol Concern, pointed out that these companies had been allowed a major say in 'setting the agenda'.[53]

There are countless other examples where governments have failed to protect the public from known risks. Take mesothelioma, a horrible and painful cancer of the lining of the lung caused by exposure to asbestos. In 1955, Richard Doll showed a clear relationship between asbestos and the pleural cancer, but it took until 1999 for the complete prohibition of the use and import of all forms of the deadly fibres and for suffering workers to be compensated.[54] Governments are culpable for such failures and delays, but public health advocates can take heart from examples where, eventually, they won out over the power of vested interests.

If children are to be protected from injury, the risks have to be understood and the public informed about them so that change can follow. Currently the public is not being informed. So the first step is to campaign for and institute proper monitoring of rugby injuries (and all sports injuries). A community-based injury surveillance system is feasible and relatively easy to implement. Rolled out across nations it would provide solid information on the risks of rugby and other sports, upon which further prevention strategies could be based. In the meantime the information that we already have needs to be provided to parents and schools, and it is hoped that this book will go some way towards this. Of course, when coming up against powerful forces, evidence on its own is not enough. The battle must also be fought through a media that is not likely to be sympathetic, given the overlapping corporate interests and commercial sponsorship at play. But most of all we must effect a change of consciousness in the public at large.

This book is both a warning about the dangers of children's rugby and a rallying cry for action. In the following pages I show just how difficult it is to get data on rugby injuries and I expose the complex nexus of interests at work to keep it that way. I describe how colleagues and I came to conduct our own survey of school rugby injuries, and in so doing we demonstrate that genuine injury surveillance is possible. Part II sets out to tackle the crucial questions to which parents need answers before letting their children play rugby. Having surveyed the academic evidence from around the world with the help of colleagues Graham Kirkwood and Nikesh Parekh, we distil the essential information to address common queries like how do the risks of rugby compare to other sports; what kinds of injury are likely; which is the most dangerous position; and can protective kit help. We give a figure for the probability that a child will be seriously injured during the rugby season and explain the method we advocate for presenting this information in a clear, understandable form to parents.

School rugby should be made safe. We know that most injuries occur as a result of contact, so there is already a strong case for restricting or abolishing the contact element of the game. Proper efforts must be made to monitor injuries and assess the danger that our children are in when they take to the rugby pitch. If all school rugby injuries were treated seriously and recorded we would soon develop a better understanding of how to prevent them. If this were to make rugby less dangerous for children then it would be a victory for parents. But if not, if it turns out that rugby cannot be played safely, and those proponents of the game are unwilling to confront the truth about contact being the cause of injury, then the case for a ban would be made. Our starting point must be the safety and well-being of our children. First do no harm.

Part I

Foul Play:
The Hidden Truth
Behind Rugby Injuries

1
Another Injury, but
Not Another Statistic

It is one of those perfect Saturday afternoons in early
autumn in Edinburgh; low sun, a cool wind blows, and
behind the high, white goal posts, the Pentland hills form
a glorious backdrop to the fine old oak and chestnut trees
sheltering the pitch. Parents gather for the weekly ritual
to watch their sons play rugby. The air resounds with
calls of 'Tackle. Tackle!' as the opposition moves the ball
swiftly out to the wing, stretching our defence. 'Take him
out', someone yells, and a flanker launches himself at the
winger's legs, bringing him down. Players pile in and suddenly the opposition's scrum half emerges with the ball and
threatens to score; but the full-back tackles him high on the
body and saves the day. It is an intensely satisfying moment
for the team and for supporters.

Until, that is, we notice that the scrum half, still a child in
the eyes of the law, stays down. Play stops. Is he concussed,
a knee ligament torn, a shoulder dislocated, or is his neck
broken? Referee and parents cluster around the still, silent

boy. Players stare anxiously, then nervously look away.
The referee takes out his mobile and dials 999. After what
seems like an age the ambulance comes to take the victim
to the Accident and Emergency department. Sometimes
the game continues even when the child is taken to hospital. Today however, the game will not play on; this time
the injury is deemed too serious. It is many rugby parents'
nightmare, and every rugby-playing boy's fear.

It is another injury but not necessarily another statistic.
Rugby is a collision sport; it involves high velocity physical
contact and the risk of injury is significant. After the scrum,
the tackle is the most dangerous phase of play, and being
the most frequent is where the majority of injuries occur.
If each game were preceded by an incantation of injury
statistics, a sombre toll of casualties from earlier games
in the season, there would be no more shouts of 'tackle,
tackle'; rather a prayer of 'take care, take care'. Unlike
road collisions, rugby injuries are not monitored and data
are not collected routinely, even though rugby-playing
schools collectively experience the equivalent of a multiple
car pile-up of traumatic injury each weekend of play. The
Scottish Rugby Union for example only requires clubs to
complete injury forms for serious injuries, those requiring hospital treatments. These statistics have only become
available since the launch in 2009 of the Are You Ready to
Play Rugby safety scheme following adverse publicity concerning child rugby injury in Scotland.[1] Because parents
are not given proper data on injury they cannot make an
informed assessment of the risks to their children. And yet
if you talk to the surgeons that repair broken cheekbones
and faces (maxilla facial surgeons) in many parts of the

country they will tell you that rugby is comparable to the Saturday night drunken brawl as one of the most common causes of smashed cheekbones and concussion.

Public health advocates operate on the premise that, in principle, every injury is preventable and avoidable. Rugby enthusiasts, on the other hand, assume that injuries are an inevitable and unavoidable part of the game. Invariably, sport-related injuries are classified as 'bad luck', and those of us who question injury rates are portrayed as 'wrapping our children in cotton wool'. But injury is not bad luck, nor a matter of chance, nor an act of God. It is inevitable for many rugby-playing children because the Laws of the Game are not constructed to prevent injury and avoid harm. We would not advocate teaching toddlers to climb by throwing them downstairs, or send a seven-year-old child alone to a hazardous road to learn to cycle, so why is it so different for children learning the game of rugby? And if other countries can closely monitor sports and rugby injuries, why not the United Kingdom, and especially Scotland which prides itself on data collection through the Information Statistics Division, one of the jewels in the crown of the country's National Health Service?

A Personal Quest for Better Data

I must confess to a conflict of interest. I have a son who has been injured three times playing rugby, all before the age of sixteen. He has suffered a broken nose, a fractured leg and a fractured cheekbone with concussion. Until he was injured, like every other parent, I trusted the school and the authorities to look after him and not expose him to the risk of serious harm. When my son started playing rugby, I did not ask about the statistics because I assumed monitoring and audit would be routine. But after my son's injuries I soon found out that the situation was not so straightforward. A few mothers urged me on, saying that as a physician and a public health professor (I was then director of the Centre for International Public Health Policy and assistant principal at the University of Edinburgh) I was well placed to uncover the facts, and that if I didn't, no-one else would. So I began my search for information about rugby's harms and benefits.

This is a story about the struggle to obtain data and statistics in order to get at the truth. I had thought it would be a relatively easy and rational exercise. My requests for information were polite and reasonable and I did not expect to be stonewalled. Nor did I expect to find reluctance on the part of the authorities and government to monitor injuries, or to discover that protecting the reputation of the game had a higher priority. But I was mistaken on all counts. The search for truth took my colleagues and me to the heart of the rugby establishment, with its close ties to government and industry, and to the centre of Scottish medicine and the University of Edinburgh.

Through the course of the search we met sustained opposition and silence. And the more we pressed for answers the more ferocious the resistance became. When my son's leg was broken in a tackle in 2004, I wrote to Scotland's deputy Chief Medical Officer (CMO) to ask about injury surveillance and to express my concerns over what seemed to me to be abnormally high rates of injury on weekends. Not a week goes by in rugby-playing schools in Scotland without a group of boys hobbling down the drive on crutches or in plaster. I was puzzled not to receive a meaningful reply or any data.

A year later, my son had his face smashed in and a cheekbone badly broken during a game. I was shocked to the core by his deformed face, his shattered cheek, his eye hanging down and his inability to eat or drink anything but liquids through a straw. Much later he would tell me that this third injury was a life-changing event that shook his confidence, affected his academic progress and other activities. He had been a keen trombonist.

In 2005, feeling negligent as a parent for not considering the risks, I wrote again to the CMO's office asking for data. I also wrote to my son's headmaster and later met with him, the sports teachers and the school's parents' association. The headmaster's response was that monitoring was the responsibility of the Scottish Rugby Union (SRU), so I wrote to the SRU and a meeting was arranged at Murrayfield in the offices overlooking the new debt-laden stadium. Here I learnt from SRU staff that there were no injury data. Apparently the secretary responsible had been ill with cancer for two years and no information had been collected or analysed. The staff also said the SRU was cash-strapped because of debt repayment on the new stadium and did not have money to employ statisticians or undertake data collection. I contacted the school again and offered to do an audit of injuries, only to be told that the injury book was missing after a move of premises and there were no records. The school later retracted this but would not give me the data.

In the summer of 2006 I decided to conduct my own

investigation and audit by telephoning every parent and school-leaver in the seventy-six-strong sixth-year of my son's school. I phoned the parents over a four-week period. I asked about the number of years children had played and the number of injuries by cause, type and phase of play. The results were surprising and alarming. Almost 37 per cent of boys had received an injury due to rugby, but the proportion of children injured increased with the level of the game. It is interesting to note that about two fifths of the boys did not like the game and had either never played or had stopped playing as soon as they could (giving the lie to the claim that the sport is universally loved and embraced). For this group, 9 per cent had been injured by the time boys had reached the age of seventeen; whereas for those playing for the first and second fifteen 70 per cent had sustained at least one serious injury involving fracture, dislocation, ligament tear or concussion since their entry into secondary school five years earlier. This compares with 43 per cent playing at a lower level. But these bare statistics do not convey the full story; some parents talked with anguish about their sons' permanent back and neck damage, of compound fractures, air ambulances, long hospital journeys, anxious, painful waits and time lost from school and education. For too many these were the indelible memories of schoolboy rugby.

I worked on the data over the summer months and sent the information in the form of a report to the headmaster. I went to speak to him, his team, and the medical doctor at the school where I was met with extraordinary hostility. I was refused permission to present my findings to the parents' forum. I suggested that alternatives to rugby

Table 1 Number and percentage of boys injured and uninjured due to rugby by level of play for the upper sixth cohort, 2001–02 to 2006–07 (number of boys = 76)

Level of play	No injuries	1 injury	≥2 injuries	Total
Not keen / stopped playing as soon as they could in the upper years	29	2	1	**32 (9%)**
Low level (third to fifth fifteen)	12	7	2	**21 (43%)**
High level (first and second fifteen)	7	7	9	**23 (70%)**
Total	**48**	**16**	**12**	76 (37%)

be introduced in lower years but this was thought to be impracticable. The headmaster informed me that he did not feel he should talk to me without a lawyer present.

In autumn 2007 I sent the results of the school audit and a brief literature review by registered post to the Chief Medical Officer, the SRU, the Health and Safety Executive, the Local Education Authority and the Children's Commissioner. There followed a flurry of phone calls expressing concern, and then silence. The problem of information collection seemed to these agencies intractable. In one respect this is understandable; rugby is only one sport while injury surveillance cuts across many departments including health, education, sport, home office and criminal justice departments. No minister and no department wanted to take responsibility.

Background to Injury: No Data, No Monitoring

Sports injury is an extraordinarily neglected area. A child can have a cancer as rare as a hen's tooth but data will be collected on each and every case, and rightly so. This does not hold for sports and rugby injuries. In this sphere public authorities are not obliged to provide sound information about the risks of injury so that teachers and schools, with a duty of care to children, can take preventative measures.

Yet schools and education authorities take special precautions to protect their wards against, for example, explosive and hazardous materials in the chemistry and physics labs; a school trip requires extraordinary vigilance by the school authority, the Health and Safety Executive and other public bodies. But sport and rugby injury has few of the public health precautions one would expect because the risks are treated differently and data are not collected. Many schools do not even enforce rules on wearing gum-shields, which are still voluntary despite compelling evidence that they prevent injury.[2]

The omission is more striking given the significance of injuries in general for child health. Injury is the principal cause of childhood mortality throughout the European Union.[3] In 2012, in Scotland, there were nineteen deaths from injuries among the under-fifteens, fifteen of which were unintentional. Excluding infants, that amounts to 23 per cent of all mortalities among boys under fifteen and 8 per cent among girls.[4] Unintentional injury is one of the common causes of emergency hospital admissions in children, accounting for 7,039 trips to Accident and Emergency (A&E) for under-fifteen-year-olds in Scotland in 2013.[5] Approximately one in seven emergency hospital admissions in children is as a result of an unintentional injury.[6] In 2007, the most recent year for which data were available, unintentional injuries are estimated to have cost the Scottish NHS £40 million, while the cost to society as a whole is thought to be around £400 million.[7]

Of non-fatal unintentional injuries in children an estimated one in five result from sport or recreational activity and almost a third occur in a place used for sport, play or recreation.[8] Across the European Union, sport is a major cause of injury, accounting for 18 per cent of all home and leisure injuries, two thirds of which happen to the under-twenty-fives.[9]

What Studies of Rugby Show

Rugby union is the most popular worldwide collision sport and participation is growing.[10] Played predominantly by men, but increasingly by women and girls, rugby has raised concerns about its physical dangers for over thirty years owing to its exceptionally physical, high-impact nature.[11] The literature suggests that too often injuries to young athletes are dismissed as 'a part of the game', rather than being seen as avoidable.[12] Physical activity in children is promoted extensively in Western countries, as it should be.[13] But the associated risks and costs of injury as a consequence of participation should not be ignored. Injuries can be expected to happen during any sporting activity; however, it is also true that a disproportionate number of injury incidents occur in rugby union relative to many other sports.[14] Exposure to this risk is not a simple matter of choice. In some schools, especially private, independent (public) schools, rugby is a compulsory part of the curriculum. Children have no option but to play, even when they do not want to.

General ignorance about the hazards of rugby is largely
due to an absence of systems able to promote monitoring
and data collection. However, individual academic studies
should ring alarm bells among teachers and parents. They
show that rugby is a high-risk game with greater rates
of serious injury than many other sports; that there is an
under-reported epidemic of concussions and head injury;
and that even mild concussion impedes educational attainment in both the short and longer term, sometimes with
catastrophic results. Every injury, whether it is a fracture,
a spinal injury, ligament damage, a dislocated shoulder, or
concussion, can impact on a child's learning, confidence,
self-esteem and long-term physical well-being.

Parents are not made aware that on the available evidence, for every season played an individual's average risk
of injury is 17 per cent or higher – that is roughly a one in
six chance of being injured in a season – and the risk accu-
mulates with exposure to play. It is highly unlikely that a
rugby-playing child will complete their schooling without
experiencing a serious rugby injury.[15]

Neither is it generally known how much more aggressive rugby has become since the sport became professional
in 1995, not only at the top level but among schoolboys.
Studies report an almost doubling in the rate of injury since
the game turned professional. Statistically, every fifty-nine
minutes a team member was injured during the 1997–8
season.[16]

In 1975, Jack Kyle, a former international rugby union
player and surgeon, said: 'Let us have no conspiracy of
silence with regard to these serious injuries or to deaths
on the rugby field. Our duty is to study the mechanisms

of injury in all phases of the game. Then, and only then, will we be able to take preventative action.'[17] Almost forty years later the conspiracy of silence endures and the monitoring systems are largely absent in the UK. This is despite medical journals, outspoken surgeons and coaches repeatedly drawing attention to the need for rugby injury surveillance over decades.

2

Rugby's Web of Interests

In 2008, following my experience with the school injury audit, my colleague Graham Kirkwood and I reviewed the academic literature and studies to prepare briefings which we presented at meetings with parliamentarians in the House of Lords, the House of Commons, and in the health and sports committee of the Scottish Parliament. There was polite interest but little action. So in March 2008, I went public with an article in the *Herald*, which described the Scottish Government's failure to ensure proper injury surveillance as 'bordering on the criminally negligent'.[1]

The main response to the piece came from the Principal of Edinburgh University, Professor Sir Timothy O'Shea. At a meeting to discuss concerns others had raised with him he drew attention to the *Herald* article and had underlined the 'criminally negligent' passage. In a letter dated 7 October 2008, he asked me to make clear that the views expressed in the article were mine alone and not the university's:

Dear Allyson,

As you know from our previous conversations on the matter, I am a great supporter of the right to academic freedom and freedom of speech, and am very pleased when academic colleagues make informed and lively contributions to matters of public policy. That said, I have decided that I should write to you following concerns raised with me recently regarding various articles and press commentary by you.

I appreciate that you have a high media profile and I am not in any way asking you to alter that. However, it is important that any views you express are your own views and you are not writing in a University of Edinburgh capacity. *I should therefore be grateful if you could ensure that this is made clear in any future articles, perhaps, for example, by inserting a sentence at the end to the effect that, '… the views expressed in this article are those of Professor Allyson Pollock and are not necessarily shared by the University of Edinburgh' or similar* [emphasis added].

I am sure you will appreciate the importance of this point and I hope you understand why I have decided to write.

Yours sincerely,

Tim

I was puzzled because unlike commercial corporations, universities do not usually try to protect themselves from the 'views' of their staff. They are places for inquiry, dissent, criticism and debate, places where academics are supposed to have the freedom to run the truth to earth. I stood my ground and after meeting with the principal to explain our work I sent him the briefings, data, a letter with a note on academic freedom and a copy of John Stuart Mill's *On Liberty*.

The Rugby Establishment

What I did not fully appreciate at the time was the complex web of interests I was confronting. Scottish rugby is rooted in the professional class that is made up of the law, finance, commerce and medicine – all products of the university system. These powerful establishment networks make the pursuit of this kind of public health extremely difficult.

Scotland is proud of its rugby heritage, not least being home to the oldest organised rugby union league in the world, the Border League.[2] According to the International Rugby Board (IRB), Scotland has 257 rugby union clubs; 96,040 pre-teen male players; 38,531 teen male players; 13,873 senior male players (total male players 148,808); 68,249 (total) female players; and 3,457 referees (as of October 2013).[3] However, many more pre-teen players are not registered with the SRU, which is a member of the IRB.

Scottish rugby has traditionally relied upon the large state and fee-paying independent schools to feed the teams. The universities are the traditional powerhouses of rugby in Scotland, and they have their own leagues; some also play in national club competitions. The University of Edinburgh is one of the top rugby-playing universities, and fields a team in the Scottish National League.[4]

The SRU oversees the Premiership, the National Leagues and the regional leagues. The Premiership is semi-professional and players can receive anything from a housing allowance to £15,000 a year plus a car. In contrast, professional rugby players in Scotland will earn in excess of £100,000 at international level (albeit small beer compared with football earnings).

The Cult of Legend and Tradition

Commerce is relatively new to the game. Rugby has its roots in folk football, a game of the masses, but the distinct history of rugby union is replete with myths and legends that served to differentiate it on class grounds: rugby union was a game for gentlemen, played by men who had no need of financial remuneration.

The story goes that in 1823 at Rugby School, a forging ground for the English establishment, a pupil named William Webb Ellis invented rugby by picking up the football during a game and running with it. The story is a myth, which, as Tony Collins explains in his marvellous book *Rugby's Great Split*, 'served to anchor rugby games as separate from the plebeian tradition of folk football, creating a middle-class lineage for the sport'.[5] 'The Great Split' in 1905 led to two forms of the game: rugby union, the gentleman's sport, which remained amateur until 1995; and rugby league, played by the working class, which became professional some one hundred years before its counterpart. Rugby School promoted the sport as a means of 'hardening' boys to imbue them with a Corinthian spirit. This notion of hardening survives to this day, as does the idea of rugby giving children 'a healthy mind in a healthy body'. In 1863 the game was described as 'an enthralling, engrossing passion that seems to madden all who come beneath its influence as the Thyrsi of Bacchus frenzied the Maenads of old'.

In Scotland, rugby is endowed with an almost sacred status. When trying to understand why parents are willing to expose their children to the risks of injury, the explanation is cultural. Male Scottish psyche, class, status, the public school system, tradition and recent commercialisation all play a part. But there is also another reason, aside from the lack of available information, why the situation is allowed to persist without a deafening outcry. This is that injuries are wrongly described by the public and policy makers as accidents, thought to be an inevitable and unpreventable aspect of life, and therefore not attributable to the game of rugby. This is simply not the case; it has been widely suggested that 90 per cent of injuries are preventable with appropriate resources.[6] It is no longer correct to refer to injuries as accidents but rather as 'unintentional injuries'. This drive to change the terminology reflects the preventable nature of injuries, as opposed to accepting them as events out of normal control.[7] However, while there is a growing recognition of the need to change the terminology of injury, the UK has still failed to find sufficient momentum to address the issue. As a signatory of the 1989 UN Convention on the Rights of the Child, the government has both a moral duty and legal obligation to prioritise injury prevention.[8]

3

A Pilot Study of Injuries

In autumn 2008, a young boy from Merchiston Castle School was rendered quadriplegic during a game of rugby in Edinburgh. Only a few months earlier another fifteen-year-old boy had been similarly injured at St Aloysius College in Glasgow. There were seven schoolboy spinal injuries in Scotland in the three years, 2007, 2008 and 2009. (We do not have the data for England, but there are more than a hundred paralysed rugby players in the UK.)[1] The number of near-catastrophic or catastrophic spinal injuries in children due to playing rugby was causing growing alarm. One month previously, I had said to the headmaster of my son's school that it was only a matter of time before another catastrophe happened. Unknown to me at the time, David Allan, the consultant in charge of the Queen Elizabeth National Spinal Injuries Unit, the leading spinal injuries unit for Scotland at the Southern General Hospital in Glasgow, had already written to the CMO (Chief Medical Officer). He was concerned by the rise in spinal

injuries caused by competitive school rugby. The SRU and
the office of the CMO simply had to act.

The first thing that happened was a change to the rules.
Under pressure to show that it was responding, the SRU
held a hasty ten-day consultation before rushing out a rule
change to bring Scotland in line with the rest of the world:
children playing rugby would have to be matched for age
and weight, so that small players would be less at risk. This
was followed by the launch of the Are You Ready to Play
Rugby? campaign in 2009, which included new minimum
coaching and refereeing standards.[2] The policy came into
effect at the start of the 2009–10 season. There has been no
subsequent evaluation of this initiative.

The CMO Harry Burns was very helpful. Previously,
in response to my repeated telephoning and briefings in
the Scottish parliament, in August 2008 he had asked Dr
Alastair Nicol, who was on secondment to his office, to
work with me in the Centre for International Public Health
Policy on an injury study. This was a very important development. Dr Nicol was a doctor with a special interest in
rehabilitation medicine and sports injury, who had spent
much of his medical career working for the army. He was
an ideal person for the job because he was passionate about
rugby and as medical adviser to the Scotland A squad
(Scotland's second national team) he was closely associated with the SRU and the players, even travelling with
them on tours. He was to be appointed later as consultant in sport medicine in the Fitness Assessment and Sports
Injury Centre (FASIC), a private clinic at the University
of Edinburgh. As Dr Nichol was not an academic and had
no previous experience of academic research, we were

delighted to arrange an appointment for him as an honorary research fellow in the Centre for International Public Health Policy so that the joint study could be conducted under my direction.

Our initial focus was on the injury monitoring forms that the SRU had intermittently collected. However, we soon found that the forms were incomplete because they were only filled in following a death or an overnight hospital stay. This approach left huge gaps in the data. In the UK, few children with even serious injuries will be admitted overnight from A&E. This meant that the majority of serious injuries, including fractures, dislocations, ligament tears, and concussion, were not recorded. Clearly, little had been done since I first met the SRU in 2005 at Murrayfield stadium to draw attention to the lack of monitoring.

With support from Dr James Robson, the Head of Medical Services at the SRU, Dr Nicol, Graham Kirkwood and I decided to conduct a pilot study in six schools to look at the feasibility of improving the form and implementing a proper injury surveillance system. The only external grant-funding involved the secondment of Dr Nicol from the CMO's office. Lack of proper funds and the short period of Dr Nicol's release meant that the study was very limited in size. Data were collected from six schools during the second half of the 2008–9 season (January to April 2009). Thanks to Dr Nicol's zealous pursuit and encouragement, the schools responded well, although one later withdrew.

Our study showed a total of thirty-seven injuries recorded over 193 matches, of which twenty required A&E attendance. The incidence of injury in competitive

school matches was 10.8 per 1,000 player-hours. The head
and face were the most commonly injured body part, and
the tackle was the phase of play where injuries were most
frequent. Sprain and ligament injury was found to be the
most common, while 65 per cent of injuries prevented
further participation in the sport for three weeks or more.
These findings were consistent with other similar studies
of school-level rugby union injuries. The problem with
these data is they did not translate into meaningful measures of risk.[3]

Of concern was the time lost from the sport with 65 per
cent of the injuries (twenty-four of the thirty-seven injuries) requiring more than three weeks away from the sport
and 13.5 per cent more than twelve weeks (see Table 2).

We concluded that the collection of reliable and relevant sports injury data in UK schools was both simple
and feasible. Consequently we advocated a rugby injury
surveillance system to be established to enable a better
understanding of the epidemiology and to inform successful injury prevention. We had shown a reliable method for

Table 2 Severity of training and match injuries, reported as time lost
from sport in study of six schools as reported by Nicol et al.: number
and percentage of injuries by injury severity (reported as number of
weeks' absence from sport) following injury[4]

Injury severity	Number of injuries	Percentage of all injuries
< 1 week	6	16.2%
1–2 weeks	7	18.9%
3–6 weeks	17	45.9%
7–12 weeks	2	5.4%
> 12 weeks	5	13.5%
Total	**37**	**100%**

data collection and had improved injury report forms so they could be easily completed for each incident.

When we followed up our research at the end of 2010, six months after publication, the SRU refused to provide details on what (if anything) was being done to improve surveillance in schools through the completion of these revised injury report forms and statistical monitoring of the resulting data.

To our surprise this small study was the first such research in eleven years anywhere in the UK. The absence of data and other studies tells a story of both neglect and complacency on the part of government and rugby unions. This alone is a cause for concern as the rugby unions had been alerted ten years before to the increasing risk of serious injury. In a meticulous and detailed follow-up to a *Lancet* study, published in the *British Journal of Sports Medicine* in 2000, Professor Michael Garraway of the University of Edinburgh and colleagues reported a near doubling in the proportion of injuries after the game became professional, with particularly high rates in school-age boys.[5] When I contacted Professor Garraway by telephone to ask why no more studies had been done and what had happened as a result of his findings, he told me he was not given further funding because his findings of the negative impact of professionalisation on injury would hurt the game's image and in his words 'the SRU could see where this was going'. The reputational stakes were too high. He told me he had had to abandon the cohort studies and further work and had destroyed the database.

The Role of Commerce and Sponsorship

Indeed, because of commercialisation the stakes are not just reputational but financial. Rugby union is increasingly driven by commercial imperatives. By 1995, football was already globalised, it was a commodity with players and clubs for sale on the world market and local team names used simply for product branding and supporter loyalty. The liberalisation of the media and television screening rights throughout the 1980s had accelerated the process. Rugby union was being left behind, and so in 1995 it relinquished its status as an amateur game for gentlemen. From media rights to sponsorship, the so-called 'adidasisation' of the sport has been well documented.

A network of commercial interests now feeds off the sport. This is clear to any visitor to Murrayfield, the home of the SRU, where advertising hoardings promote private healthcare companies BUPA and SPIRE, Emirates Airlines, security firm G4S and fund managers Murray. One sponsor is particularly interesting: the logo of the Royal Bank of Scotland (RBS) is emblazoned on the pitch. The RBS, which at the height of the 2008 financial crisis had to be bailed out by the British taxpayer to the tune of £46 billion and is 81 per cent publicly-owned, nevertheless announced a £20 million sponsorship deal for the Six Nations rugby union tournament in 2009 and a three-year deal with the SRU in 2010.[6] Even though the bank is owned by the public, the details of these contracts remain confidential. RBS has thought nothing of diverting taxpayer's money to prop up rugby and the public has had no say.

Despite this inflow of cash, most rugby unions including the SRU have run up significant debts. Huge investments in large stadia and players can only be paid for with more commercial sponsorship, public funds, aggressive marketing, the sale of land and an expanded support base. But over the last five years, while the SRU has sought to reduce accumulated debts that peaked at £25 million in 2003–4, ticket sales have fallen. Rugby is envious of football, where some teams can command more than 40,000 supporters at each match, compared with a few thousand for local rugby teams.

To help the sport grow, discounted tickets are offered to schoolchildren. The SRU is targeting schoolboys, schoolgirls, and club rugby to create a new generation of players, coaches, referees and supporters. A new Academy structure has been established 'to raise the standard of elite play by providing a strong and reliable flow of the best young talent,' starting at the under-sixteen level.[7] Some independent schools are now offering rugby scholarships to poor children in deprived areas as part of the requirement to demonstrate public benefit for tax purposes. Above all, government sponsorship is seen as vital to restore and maintain SRU's financial position.

4

Marginalizing the Causes
of Public Health

Early in 2009, with the addition to our team of Nikesh Parekh, a young medical student, we were able to push ahead with a parallel study focusing on the way in which injury data is presented. I asked Nikesh to review international studies of rugby injuries in schoolchildren and examine why many of the studies were largely impossible for a layperson to interpret. The problem arose from the practice of reporting epidemiological data as 'injury per player-exposure period', an approach that did not show the actual risk of injury. We reasoned that parents and teachers would find estimates of risk more intelligible. Calculating the period of exposure was likely to be misleading because the number of injuries per player-hour was not a meaningful statistic. We wanted to transform data such as 'ten injuries per 1,000 player-hours' into an understandable risk figure that would help to explain to parents, teachers and children the probability of injury.

Nikesh Parekh asked Professor Stewart Hodges from

the Cass Business School in London to work with him on converting the data into probability statistics – to explain what the risk or chance of injury is. This is normal practice in occupational medicine as well as health and safety in the workplace, but not in sports medicine. The results of our small study showed that the risk of injury is as follows: assuming that the average schoolboy would play fifteen matches in a season with each game lasting for seventy minutes, the incidence of injury converts to a 17 per cent likelihood of the player sustaining an injury in such a typical season (or roughly a one in six chance). For this calculation, injury is defined as any complaint that prevents participation in sport for at least one week, a so-called 'time-loss injury'. This is exactly the sort of information parents, children and teachers need.[1]

Our work on rugby injuries was beginning to attract media attention. One journalist in particular, Mark Macaskill of the *Sunday Times*, showed a tenacious interest in data collection and injury surveillance and followed our work closely. The rest of the media also began to give rugby injuries some coverage in documentaries and television programmes.

By the end of 2009, the pilot study and literature review were complete and were being written up for publication. In July 2010 Mark Macaskill announced the research in the *Sunday Times* under the banner headline 'Leading public health researcher calls for ban on scrum and high tackle'. The news story reverberated around the world, with over a hundred press reports. A small study had made a great deal of impact.[2]

I was unprepared for the backlash in Scotland. The

SRU took offence to my call for changes to the Laws of
the Game and claimed that I had exceeded the evidence
from the study. Offensive emails from rugby players and
officials filled my inbox. Rugby academics funded by
rugby unions pitched in to defend the sport, including Ken
Quarrie (senior scientific injury researcher for the New
Zealand Rugby Union), who accused me of 'crying wolf',
although he had clearly failed to read the scientific paper
or the interviews properly and had not acquainted himself
with the appalling state of injury collection in Scotland
and the UK.[3] (There were others who called for a proper
debate.) Rugby research funded by rugby unions is a closed
shop, and research is often carefully crafted to obscure the
evidence, with a few notable exceptions such as the recent
work on English community rugby by Simon Roberts and
on professional players by John Brooks.[4]

In claiming that our study did not support a rule change,
the SRU was choosing to ignore the wider scientific literature to which the study had drawn attention. This literature
shows that injuries are frequent and the probability and risk
of injury are high; that injuries are more common early in
the season; and that tackle and scrum are vulnerable phases
of play. As Garraway et al. wrote in the *British Journal of
Sports Medicine* in 2000:

> Many injuries occur in the tackle in both codes but changes in
> the laws of rugby union in recent years have been designed
> to encourage more open play. This has probably resulted in
> more tackles involving a higher degree of momentum or the
> use of greater force. Tackles coming in at high speed from
> behind the tackled player have recently been highlighted as
> an important factor in injuries occurring in rugby union.

Changes in the Laws of the Game which have come into force since the first survey was carried out during the 1993–4 season may have played a part in the major increase in the rate of injuries which have occurred in both professional and amateur players.[5]

Serious rugby experts and commentators have called in the pages of the *British Medical Journal* (BMJ) and the national media for revisions to the Laws of the Game, including a ban on the scrum.[6] This thoughtful review written by James Bourke in 2006 in the BMJ is worth quoting in full:

Rugby union should ban contested scrums.

For thirty years I have been an honorary medical officer to Nottingham Rugby Football Club. In this time I have attended about twenty-five games a season and on many occasions have been the 'duty doctor,' either officially or unofficially. In that time four players have been removed from the field of play at Nottingham with serious neck injuries. Three of the injuries were associated with scrums, and one occurred in a tackle. All four players had initial sensory and motor impairment. Two recovered within minutes or hours; one recovered in days; and one became paraplegic. Three needed an operation for fracture. Another three Nottingham players injured their necks in scrums while playing away from home and needed to be removed from the pitch. One player needed an operation and is paraplegic. Therefore I have experience of seven serious spinal cord injuries, five of which have required an operation. Two of the players are wheelchair dependent. Six of the seven injuries were related to the scrum, and in all cases the scrums were of the contested type – in which each set of forwards tries to shove the opponents off the ball – and that is more dangerous than the uncontested scrum, in which the

players are not allowed to push their opponents away from
the spot where the scrum occurs.

The continuing risk of injury cannot be accepted.

A recent Australian study looked at acute spinal cord injuries among players of rugby union, rugby league, Australian
rules football, and soccer from 1997 to 2002.[7] These data
were compared with those from a 1986–96 survey. Fifty-two
players (forty-five men and seven schoolboys) suffered acute
spinal cord injuries over the study period. The average annual
incidence of such injuries per 100,000 players was 3.2 for
rugby union, 1.5 for rugby league, 0.5 for Australian rules,
and 0.2 for soccer. Although the incidence had changed little
since the earlier survey, there was a trend towards less severe
injuries in rugby union and league but not in Australian rules.
No scrum injuries have occurred in rugby league in Australia
since 1996, when contested scrums stopped being allowed.
Seven injuries occurred in rugby union scrums, six at the
moment of engagement with the opposing team. Overall 39
per cent of injured players became permanently dependent
on a wheelchair. The Australian authors also noted that the
cost of care of a quadriplegic young man over his lifetime
is enormous. For a nineteen-year-old with C5 quadriplegia
resulting from a road traffic crash in 2002 the payout would
be between $A7m (£3m; $5.4m) and $A9m. They say that
under the existing insurance cover for rugby union players,
however, the maximum award for quadriplegia is $A300,000.
The study concludes that the laws of scrum engagement in
rugby union and the amount of insurance cover for injured
players are grossly inadequate.

In Britain acute spinal cord injuries in rugby union continue to occur, typically associated with scrums at the moment
of engagement. Wheelchair dependency among those injured
is common, and insurance is inadequate. The rugby football

union is known to be concerned about the high level of injury, severity, and insurance.

Rugby union became professional in 1995; players are paid to play and train. Professional rugby union is now often described as an industry. It may be subject to the Health and Safety at Work Act (1974), which requires working practices that are safe and do not put workers at risk. In the under-nineteen game contested scrums are not allowed.

The authors of the 2005 Australian paper noted: 'In our opinion there has been a gradual return to a forceful scrum engagement. While this may allow a tactical advantage for a team, it increases the risk of engagement injury. In our present study six of the seven scrum injuries occurred at engagement. We recall the 1988 warning of Burry and Calcinai of the need to make rugby safer – that "failing to alter the procedures of a game despite the knowledge that existing practices were hazardous and a safe alternative existed could well be held by a court to constitute culpable negligence".'[8]

In Britain such a case went to court in 2002: that of Richard Vowles of the Llanharan second XV against the Welsh Rugby Union. Vowles had suffered a severe injury in a game in January 1998 that left him paralysed when the players in the scrum failed to engage properly. The court ordered the Union to compensate Vowles.

The incidents involving the two young Nottingham players who are now wheelchair dependent have caused me to change my opinion on contested scrums. The consequences of injury are so great that the continuing risk of injury cannot be accepted.

Players now deserve uncontested scrums in rugby union. In rugby league in Australia no acute spinal cord injuries have occurred since the scrum stopped being contested. Rugby union should follow this example. Rugby union outlawed the 'flying wedge' and the 'cavalry charge' as they are potentially dangerous. It should now also outlaw the contested scrum.

James B Bourke, consultant general surgeon.[9]

Unfortunately the SRU was more interested in public relations than in responding to the facts. Its strategy focused on how to restrict comment on the findings of our small pilot study and not on the general body of research evidence. Professor Garraway, writing in the *British Journal of Sports Medicine* in 2000, noted similar preoccupations:

> The principal concerns of the IRB in adopting professionalism have been to establish the sport's commercial viability and adapt organisational structures to manage it. More emphasis should now be placed on players' health and welfare.[10]

Dr Nichol, with his close involvement with the SRU as its appointed medical adviser to the Commonwealth Games in Delhi, was feeling the heat. In July 2010 he emailed me to say he was unhappy with the press coverage and would not support any criticism of the SRU, even though I had no control over how the press reported the story. Regrettably, without consulting me or other study members he then wrote a letter to the *Herald* on 8 July 2010 and an editorial in the *Scotsman* distancing himself from the Centre and our research:

> Dear Editor,
>
> In recent press reports, Professor Allyson Pollock of Edinburgh University has cited a newly published study on injuries in school rugby to support her claim that scrums in school and youth rugby should be banned.

Having reviewed the press reports I, as the lead author of this study, am disappointed at the way in which the results have been inaccurately used as a springboard to launch an unwarranted attack on rugby.

The intention of the study was very clear – to test the feasibility of collecting injury data in schools. For that reason it only included a sample of five schools, albeit playing a total of 193 matches. With better data collection, we can learn more about risk factors to allow national bodies such as Scottish Rugby to consider initiatives which will continue to make the sport safer.

Referring specifically to the call by Professor Pollock to ban scrums, I would note that in our study there were only two injuries in the scrum, one a knee and one a back injury. Both were back playing within a few weeks. In no way can that be considered sufficient evidence to call for a ban on scrums in schools rugby.

Our paper does not make any recommendation for banning or changing the laws around the scrum. As for the tackle, it is recognised that this is the phase of play associated with most injuries. Only one injury in this study was due to an illegal (penalised) tackle. Hardly a strong case to call for an end of high tackles when they are banned already.

Rugby remains a contact sport, so there will invariably be some unavoidable injuries. Our aim is to keep them to an absolute minimum through knowledge and evidence, while encouraging those that want to play rugby to play in a safe and enjoyable environment. Scottish Rugby is to be congratulated on taking a lead on player safety and many other sports' governing bodies could do well to follow their example.

Scottish Rugby has been at the forefront of piloting a number of variations to the game's laws designed to make the game safer and more enjoyable. In fact, in 2009, Scottish

Rugby was commended by Scotland's Chief Medical Officer, Dr Harry Burns, and the International Rugby Board (IRB), for its groundbreaking introduction of the 'Are you ready to play rugby?' initiative.

Player safety remains the paramount consideration for all and Scottish Rugby has taken positive steps in recent seasons to evolve the game to ensure it remains fun and as safe as realistically possible for all.

I hope this letter provides you and your readers with a more reasoned and balanced update on player safety as opposed to the somewhat sensational comments recently seen.

Kind regards,

Dr Alastair M Nicol[11]

By choosing to focus on the number of individual injuries rather than the overall findings of the study, Dr Nichol had failed to consider how these data related and contributed to several decades of evidence that showed the high rates of injury in the game.

The Establishment Closes In: Curtailing Academic Freedom

The University of Edinburgh was also feeling the pressure. On 12 July 2010 the Principal wrote asking me to comment on a letter he had received from Dominic Mackay, the SRU's head of media and communications, in which Dr Nichol's views were cited. Mr Mackay accused me of misrepresentation and damaging the reputations of the University and the SRU. 'Prof. Pollock's comments to the media', he wrote, 'have misrepresented the findings of the study and have caused significant damage to the standing and reputation of the game in Scotland.' He called for me to be disciplined, asking the Principal 'what action you intend to take to ensure the good reputation of the University is not further damaged by those linked to Edinburgh University.'

In my note of reply to the Principal's office I attached a volume of academic evidence summarising the risks. I was therefore surprised when the Principal wrote back to Mr Mackay supporting his charge of misrepresentation on 5 August 2010:

Dear Mr McKay,

Thank you for your letter of 9 July regarding the press coverage of the recent study into rugby injuries among schoolchildren published in the *Journal of Public Health*.

I understand that this has arisen from publication of a study of which Dr Alastair Nicol was lead author, and that Professor Pollock was also involved in authorship of this report. I further understand that Dr Nicol and Professor Pollock take different views on the implications of the findings of this study.

It is not uncommon for different views to be taken in such circumstances, and sometimes these can be strongly held. The University does not take a position on such matters, but rather it encourages proper academic debate with a view to resolution of points of difference. The University would defend the right of its academic staff to express their views in such circumstances provided always that these are based upon firm evidence and rigorous and objective scholarship.

On this basis I would assure you that the views set out by Professor Pollock in the articles you refer to are entirely her own and do not represent the views of the University of Edinburgh.

University staff and students have a long history of engaging with rugby, and we are proud to have produced some fine Scottish internationals. We encourage students who so wish to participate in the game, and our Rugby Club receives strong support from our Centre for Sport and Exercise and the University Sports Union. We are pleased and proud to work with partner organisations in promoting participation in sports and the development of young talent, not least in rugby, and would very much wish that this positive working relationship continues in the future.

I hope you find this reply helpful.

Yours sincerely,

Timothy

The close relationship between the University and the SRU outlined in the closing paragraph of the Principal's letter was not at that time known to me. Had it been I would not have been so unprepared for the sinister turn that events later took – events that would strike at the very principle of academic freedom.

The University of Edinburgh, the SRU, and the Private Health Care Industry

The University of Edinburgh provides a commercial service to the SRU through its Centre for Sport and Exercise, which houses the private sports injury clinic FASIC.[12] As its website reveals, FASIC employs physiotherapists and NHS medical consultants, many of whom were trained and worked, or still work, in the NHS. These doctors and physiotherapists provide private treatment and care to students, the public and the national rugby squad. Many act as advisers for the SRU and travel with the Scottish international team during the annual Six Nations tournament, as well as going to the Olympics and Commonwealth Games. In fact the private health care industry is expanding its interests across Scotland partly through a complex network comprising academia, research, business and sport. The sector overall has close links with the SRU, the University of Edinburgh, and the local NHS. The focus on sport and exercise as health promotion activities has provided the University with potential new income streams. Students now complain about the high costs of using gym and sports facilities, which were once available for a nominal amount in the 1970s and 1980s. They are also being persuaded to pay for sports physiotherapies in private clinics operated by the University, which should be available under the NHS free at the point of delivery. Sport has carved out a private health care market for itself.

Although the NHS in Scotland eschews private medicine and the Scottish Government says it stands for a public health service, the University of Edinburgh has been quick to exploit private opportunities. The replacement of the publicly owned Royal Infirmary of Edinburgh, an NHS teaching hospital with close ties to the University, was achieved through the private finance initiative (PFI). This method of funding the construction of the hospital on private credit has left the Infirmary with an astronomically high annual charge to pay, inflated by exorbitant interest rates and the need to pay returns to shareholders. The affordability gap, as it is called – the gap between what the public can afford and what is being charged – is being squared by closing NHS services and expanding privately-funded hospital care. One member of the PFI consortium happens to be the RBS, which despite being publicly owned is still extracting public funds from the NHS and sponsoring SRU.

But that is not all: as part of the PFI deal, the health service had to sell off other hospitals and facilities, some of them on prime city-centre land. One such sale was the Gogarburn Hospital site near Edinburgh Airport, bought by none other than the RBS for a derisory sum. The bank's new headquarters is now housed there in a £340 million development. The PFI deal has not had such an agreeable outcome for the NHS, where the high cost of the debt has led to service cuts, the closure of community health and mental health facilities and a shortage of acute beds as more than a third have been lost.[13]

The University has found ways of exploiting the resulting NHS shortages, creating commercial opportunities for itself and for private medicine. For example, the private hospital chain Spire Healthcare has formed a partnership with the University of Edinburgh Medical School under which the University supplies NHS junior doctors to work in Spire hospitals. In return Spire pays their salaries and allows them time to work on research projects with NHS and university academics.[14] Spire recently opened a hospital in the grounds shared by the new PFI Royal Infirmary of Edinburgh and the University's BioQuarter.[15] This strategy of 'co-location' allows Spire to also draw on NHS doctors working in the Royal Infirmary to staff its own private services.

Spire Healthcare was formed after the sale of BUPA Hospitals to Cinven in 2007. As of 2013, it has thirty-seven private hospitals throughout the UK, employs over 7,600 people and treats over 930,000 patients per year. However, it is reliant on NHS staff, educated and trained at the public's expense, and depends on work handed out by the health service as part of waiting list initiatives – an example of the heavy public subsidy to the private health care sector.[16] In fact Spire's expansion in Edinburgh could be interpreted as a clear response to the aforementioned shortage of NHS beds in the Lothian Health Board area.[17] The company uses part of its earnings to sponsor the SRU; its name is on advertising hoardings around the Murrayfield pitch. At the same time it generates income by providing private treatment for rugby players using orthopaedic surgeons and physiotherapists, many of whom trained in and are also employed by the NHS.

This complex web of institutional interests is bound together by cross-cutting personal ties within the rugby establishment. Some NHS doctors who also carry out private practice in Spire hospitals give up their spare time to act as SRU medical attendants during games. In return they get free tickets, hospitality and sometimes travel with the squad. Doctors with academic leanings accept government funds and SRU or International Rugby Board grants to conduct research into the mechanics of the game.

Medical Conflicts of Interest

These relationships raise questions about the role of doctors in this pressurised environment. Are they medical advisers to the players, to the team or to the rugby unions? In whose interests are they acting when they provide care?

This question became pertinent in summer 2010 as the reputation of English rugby was badly tarnished by extensive media coverage of the 'Bloodgate' affair, when a doctor and a physiotherapist went before their professional bodies on a charge of deliberately inflicting harm on a rugby player, albeit at his request.[18] The doctor, Wendy Chapman, told the General Medical Council that in the closing minutes of a Heineken Cup quarterfinal tie she had been pressured by player Tom Williams to cut an incision in his lip after he had faked a blood injury by biting into a capsule. His withdrawal from the pitch had allowed a specialist goal kicker to replace him. A subsequent inquiry led to heavy fines and bans for the disgraced player and the club's director of rugby. The physiotherapist, Steph Brennan, was struck off by the Health Professions Council for 'premeditated' and 'dishonest' conduct after admitting to a total of five instances of faking blood injuries.[19] Wendy Chapman was not struck off but allowed to continue practising on the grounds of previous ill health. The practice of medicine is predicated upon the oath to do no harm. With Bloodgate the opposite was true. It is not hard to see how commercial pressures increase the likelihood of such conflicts of interests.

5

The Indemnity Question

In mid-July 2010, without warning, the Centre for International Public Health Policy webpage and its publications were taken down. For many months thereafter and until I left the university, my own website could not be found, despite repeated requests for it to be restored. Internal academic debate was also closed down. On 18 July 2010, some six days after the Principal had written to me (see above), the editor of the University staff newsletter wrote to me and Dr Nichol inviting 800 words from us both on the rugby injury story in what was to be a three-page opinion section consisting of contrasting pieces from academics. But in mid-August, the story was pulled on the instruction of Jim Aitken, director of the University's Centre for Sports and Exercise. I was told this in an email from the press officer stating that 'it would be unwise to draw attention to the issue following the press coverage' and that 'it was Jim Aitken who requested that the article should not be followed up.' The press officer was not aware that the Principal had written to me. Was it a coincidence that at Mr Aitken's invitation (made presumably at the behest of the Principal) Prince Philip, then vice-chancellor of the University, was in the same month to open a new £5 million extension at the University of Edinburgh's Pleasance Gym, described as 'one of the best gyms on the planet' by the All Blacks rugby team?[1] Mr Aitken certainly has strong links to the SRU and FASIC.

In June 2010 Jim Aitkin made the Queen's Birthday Honours list, receiving an MBE.[2] Honours and funds were being handed out to the game's supporters. In autumn 2010, Scotland's orthopaedic surgeons nominated James Robson, the medical doctor for the SRU, to a highly respected fellowship of the Royal College of Surgeons, and he was made a fellow in 2011.[3]

Separately, a group of surgeons, all fellows of the Royal College of Surgeons, was funded by the SRU to research rugby injuries and neck and body strength in schoolboys. Several of the surgeon researchers belonged to a rugby injuries subgroup convened by the Scottish Committee for Orthopaedics and Trauma (SCOT), and some also worked for Spire.[4] Several of the surgeons were also keen support-ers of rugby. (As an aside, the problem with schoolboy rugby is not boys' neck strength, but the way the game is played. Focusing on a child's individual characteristics is rather like blaming a cyclist injured in a car accident for having weak ankles or arms.)[5]

Throughout the autumn of 2010 the IRB promoted its injury prevention programme, 'Rugby Ready'. Dr Nicol and the SRU wrote to assure me of the importance the SRU attached to injury surveillance. However, information collection was still deficient and they could not provide any evidence of monitoring. This was despite the fact that the SRU, as a member of the IRB, has a responsibility to ensure that any injury needing a hospital visit is documented via a Scottish Rugby Serious Injury Report Form. It seemed surveillance and monitoring were well and truly off the agenda.

A Lone Parent Raises the Indemnity Question

As 2010 wore on, it became clear we had exhausted every avenue and silence prevailed. But in September, out of the blue, I received a phone call from Bridget Broad whose son, an amateur player, had been badly hurt during a rugby game and required surgery. Mrs Broad was concerned that her son, who had been advised of an eighteen-month wait for NHS care, had no choice but to pay to go private at a cost of £9,000 in order to return to work as a gamekeeper. In going private the family discovered that the SRU's indemnity insurance was limited to catastrophic cover that did not extend to Mrs Broad's son's injury, as it 'was available only to professional sports people through the NHS'.[6] Both clubs and players, it turned out, were under-insured. A tenacious New Zealander passionate about rugby, Mrs Broad went to the SRU to raise concerns about the lack of insurance and liability cover, the denial of care through the NHS, and the failure to complete rugby injury forms, of which she now had direct evidence. She also raised questions about the SRU's and Dr James Robson's failure to respond to her concerns and reports that injury data were not being properly collected and monitored. Her letters to

Dr Robson about the failures and lack of injury monitoring were ignored.

The indemnity question is a headache for the SRU because how can the scale of indemnity insurance be calculated when the risks of injury are unknown? Perhaps as a consequence, this is an area that has not yet been associated with much research. Those engaged in studies of rugby are often passionate about the sport. While they have conducted many vitally important studies, albeit often sponsored by the rugby unions, thorny questions about indemnity and medical liability have not been addressed.

The Medical and Dental Defence Union (MDDUS) has grappled with these questions. It provides protection to doctors against medical negligence lawsuits. It also provides cover to doctors who do 'Good Samaritan' deeds, for example tending to someone who has collapsed in the road. But what about doctors who are on hand at rugby games? These club doctors are not Good Samaritans; they are contracted to clubs by virtue of receiving payments in kind in the form of spectator boxes, free tickets and so on. Indeed, the MDDUS recently withdrew indemnity for sports medicine and reduced cover for football's Premier League. It reasoned that liability would be huge if a doctor under contract was to declare fit a player worth £30 million who was subsequently injured.[7]

Indemnity insurance is related to risk. In the US, assessments of risk have driven indemnity reform and compensation, especially in the case of American Football. In the UK, it is ironic that in the absence of risk data one of the country's biggest insurers, AVIVA, is the title-sponsor of the English Rugby Premiership, with a four-year deal worth £20 million.[8] Actuaries and insurance companies go to great lengths to estimate risks for house and car insurance, resulting in, for example, prohibitively expensive car insurance premiums for young men and older people. It is somewhat galling to know that the money they make goes into sponsoring a sport where the risks of injury are not properly monitored, especially in respect of children.

Of course, the SRU's main insurance problems are centred on the professional game rather than club and school rugby. But in Scotland, all schools are covered under the SRU insurance scheme.[9] In England all clubs and rugby-playing schools are expected to be insured either through the Rugby Football Union (RFU) or a comparable policy. However, the RFU policy only covers death and total permanent disability![10] In a 2003 paper by the Medico-Legal Society it was advised that 'players themselves would do well to insure themselves for personal accident and injury'.[11] The effect of this is to pass the risks and costs back to children and their parents, raising the question of when there is a responsibility upon the statutory body to inform them about the potential hazards of playing rugby. Seriously under-insured amateur players must take on the risks themselves.

When catastrophic and very serious injuries occur there is always the question of liability. In theory, in countries that have a universal and well-developed welfare state, long-term injuries are covered by public health, social care and benefits systems. Of course in practice this is not entirely true and many costs are externalised to the victims of injury and their families. But elsewhere, the catastrophic costs of injury, disability, and consequent unemployment have to be borne by individuals and families, often plunging them into poverty and debt.

Litigation

Medical litigation is one route towards determining where the duty of care lies and who carries the risk. It can also be a mechanism for improving safety. But in the case of rugby injury, litigation has not brought clarity.[12] Although there have been High Court actions resulting in personal awards, case law does not appear to have shaped injury policies.

One problem in the UK is that although injured players are sometimes forced to resort to legal remedy, too often cases are settled out of court and so questions of law and liability are not answered. However there is some case law. A decision in 2007, from the English Court of Appeal, held a schoolmaster and his school liable for an injury sustained by a fourteen-year-old in a competitive under-fifteen game. The case brought the complexity of liability in school injuries to light. The boy broke his elbow from a legal tackle by an opposition player who was older than fifteen, which the schoolmaster (who was also the referee) claimed to be unaware of. Ignorance was no excuse in the eyes of the law; the teacher had a duty of care. Under guidelines issued by the English Rugby Football Schools' Union, the opposition player was ineligible to play, as he was not in the right age category for the game. The practice of 'playing down' or 'playing up' schoolboys by age, size and experience and level of play is probably more common than people imagine.[13]

The threat of litigation is not something to be taken lightly by schools and governing bodies. It is of concern that a legal tackle from a player who was not significantly bigger in size could result in a schoolboy breaking his elbow. It raises the question of whether governing bodies need to consider changes to the laws of the youth game in order to better protect young players. Two cases appeared in Australia, in 2000 and 2002, of players suing a sport governing body in New South Wales for insufficient regulation of rugby union resulting in an unnecessary risk of serious injury and a breach of the duty of care. Neither case won, but both ended up in court. In Britain, a Medico-Legal Society paper published in 2003 argued that it is no defence that an injured player consented to the risk of injury.[14]

Indeed the concept of informed consent for youth participation in sports is problematic. It requires risk data to be available and presented in a meaningful way, and currently it is not. Even if it were, would school children have the maturity to fully understand the nature and magnitude of injury risks and consequences in order to make a reasoned decision? And then, even if the player gives informed consent, it can only apply to injuries that occur within proper conduct of the game and under the guidelines that governing bodies provide to schools to ensure the safety of young players.[15] Where participation in rugby is compulsory, the issue of consent becomes irrelevant, as consent implies a voluntary choice.[16] It is the role of the law to protect the vulnerable from harmful risks.

Learning from Other Countries

In rugby-loving New Zealand and Australia some health ministers have made injury surveillance a priority, and weight, age and height matching is par for the course in schoolboy rugby. A survey of Australian parents found rugby to be the sport most frequently discouraged due to concerns over safety and injury risk. In New Zealand high injury rates drove improvements to the rules of rugby.[17] The government was forced to act after three young boys were rendered quadriplegic in one weekend in 1974. I was told by a lawyer that the costs of care nearly bankrupted the New Zealand Accident Compensation Corporation (ACC). Established to prevent costly medical litigation and to ensure no-fault compensation, the ACC fund was badly depleted by catastrophic spinal injuries in men and boys, which are the tip of the iceberg of spinal and other injuries.[18] Nowadays the ACC operates a comprehensive sports injury surveillance system, which has contributed to New Zealand becoming a world leader in sports injury prevention. As the ACC has to pay the compensation for sports injuries there is a strong financial incentive to prevent them, hence the priority accorded to the issue.

Unlike New Zealand, the UK does not have an equivalent to the ACC, nor is there proper monitoring of all spinal injuries. Instead, the victims of catastrophic spinal injuries, if they do not have private insurance cover, must rely in large part on charitable support for long-term care from organisations like the Hearts and Balls charity and the RFU Injured Players foundation, which raises funds for victims of serious spinal injuries due to rugby.[19] The paradox is that while the SRU claims that there is not a problem of spinal injuries, it actively supports Hearts and Balls, a charity dedicated to it.

Why should charity be necessary? Catastrophic injury cover is insufficient when the cost of services for quadriplegia runs into tens of millions for each child damaged and must be met by the NHS, social services, housing and welfare budgets. Some essential services for victims are chargeable – for example the annual cost of social services as well as specially adapted housing, equipment and cars. However, for non-catastrophic injuries there is usually no cover to meet these costs or an insufficient pay-out where cover exists. Patients rely on the NHS, which is as it should be, but even here they can find themselves falling through the gaps and having long waits for urgent surgical care and rehabilitation. In England some clubs pay the costs of private medical care, but not all.

6

The Cost of Injuries

Mrs Broad's evidence did not just relate to the question of indemnity; she also had direct evidence of the deficiency of the injury form system. The day she and her son found themselves in A&E there were five other boys present with concussion and other injuries. One case of concussion was so severe the player was, in Mrs Broad's words, 'away with the fairies'. Not one of the forms was completed or returned and the boy with concussion went back to play a week later. Concussion guidelines insist that a boy is assessed and does not return to play for at least three weeks.

Bridget Broad met with the SRU and her Member of the Scottish Parliament, Murdo Fraser. The minutes of the meeting are revealing. They show the SRU playing down her concerns and disparaging my work and the Centre for International Public Health Policy's research, which they claimed was not supported by academic peers.

Mrs Broad's concern spurred me into once more writing and emailing the SRU to ask for the details of their surveillance system, audit and monitoring. They first ignored my emails and then refused to give me the information. I followed up by email on 18 November 2010, saying that if I did not receive a reply I would write to the CMO and the responsible government minister.

Dear Colin,

As you are aware, almost two years ago we conducted a pilot study of rugby injuries in 5/6 schools in order to improve surveillance of children and made recommendations around the improvement of the form and information gathering and audit and monitoring.

I was told we were knocking on an open door and improvements in surveillance would result. I have been knocking for a long time.

This is a follow-up email and part of ongoing academic enquiry and scrutiny in respect of our findings and the public health.

I am sure parents and children and schools and health boards will not be impressed by this response and that you are refusing to provide details of injury surveillance and monitoring or to communicate in an open and transparent way.

Is this an official response, it is not clear to me who the 'we' is? Did you send my email to Graham Ireland (SRU secretary) as requested?

If I do not have a more engaged and positive response by the end of the week I will write to the Chair of the Health and Sport Committee, the Minister concerned and the Chief Medical Officer.

Sincerely,

Allyson

On 19 November 2010, Colin Thomson, the head of community rugby for the SRU, declined to give me the information, asked for my terms of reference, and cited the SCOT committee as working on injury surveillance monitoring and the development of policies on player safety. He added: 'Scottish Rugby will be writing under separate cover to Edinburgh University to clarify the Universities [sic] position on this and in particular the threatening nature of your last email. For clarity this communication has been discussed with all Scottish Rugby staff you reference in earlier communication.'

On 25 November, I wrote again to express serious concerns about the SRU's refusal to release details of rugby injury surveillance among school children, and the next day I wrote to the CMO, and copied to the ministers of Sport, Health and Education, as follows:

Dear Harry,

Rugby injury surveillance among schoolchildren.

I am writing to express serious concerns about the Scottish Rugby Union's refusal to release to public health academics details of rugby injury surveillance among school children.

As you know, over the years I have repeatedly asked the SRU for information about injury surveillance data and systems, to little or no avail. Over the last few months I have repeated these requests, but the information has not been made available. During the summer, the head of media and communications at the SRU wrote to the Principal of this university to complain about publication of my concerns, and now its head of community rugby has said he will make a further complaint.

The SRU is in receipt of public funds, including NHS

funds in support of public health promotion activities. It has a duty of care to the whole community of players, including a duty to protect children from harm, in a sport that has become much more dangerous since professionalisation. In recent correspondence the SRU has indicated that it "does not believe it is appropriate" to release the relevant information. However, injury is a public health issue and injury surveillance should not be a private matter for the SRU.

In the light of the SRU's actions, and because of the gravity of the public health issues, the implications for indemnity insurance cover, and the need to address the potential for commercial conflicts in public health surveillance, I am notifying you again of my concerns. I have in the past raised the issue of the paucity of injury surveillance in general with you, and with government and other bodies. Scotland, in common with England and Northern Ireland, lags behind other European countries with respect to injury surveillance. Injuries are a major cause of morbidity among children, and sports injuries in older children make a significant contribution. Given the health and safety issues, and the costs of injuries to children and the NHS, a public community and hospital surveillance system to ensure monitoring and enable effective prevention strategies is long overdue. It is my view that the Scottish Government should take the lead in this. Only with proper monitoring and injury surveillance can effective prevention strategies be implemented to ensure active and safe participation in sports.

Because of the cross-cutting issues associated with injury surveillance I am copying this to the relevant ministers, departments, and agencies for information.

On 7 February 2011, the CMO replied by email:

Allyson,

Sorry for the delay in replying. [...]

After your letter, I went to see the SRU and I found them to be very open with their data. They shared the results of the injury study with me. We discussed the limitations of any such data collection projects and the various difficulties and biases that might arise. They also showed me the data relating to the assessment system they have introduced for boys wanting to play at more senior levels. This data included numbers on those who have applied, the test results and the numbers whose applications had been turned down.

They believe they have a good story to tell and are exploring how best to make the data public. I have suggested to them that I find an academic sports medicine specialist to work with them on this.

I think their system of data collection could be made more automated using ISD and, we should extend it to other contact sports. These discussions are in hand.

I saw no signs of reticence on their part and they have agreed to let me know when they feel the data is ready to be made public

Harry

Four years later in 2014, we are still waiting for the good story the SRU has to tell and the data that goes with it.

How the Scottish Government uses Taxpayer Funds to Subsidise Rugby Union

These issues should be of direct concern to the Scottish Government not just because of the safety implications, but because rugby union is subsidised with considerable amounts of public money. The SRU does not publish an account of the sources of income that recently allowed it to tackle its mounting debts or to pay for the stadium, but what is clear is that rugby has found new economic opportunities in the shape of public and government money through heritage and lottery funds and grants from bodies like Sport Scotland. The SRU is in receipt of nearly one and a half million pounds of taxpayers' money annually from the Scottish Government, and National Lottery Funds invested about £4 million from 2005–8.[1] Sport Scotland is the national agency that coordinates this funding, responsible to the Scottish Parliament through ministers. Its former head for six years was none other than Jim Aitken MBE, the head of the University of Edinburgh's Centre for Sport and Exercise, of which FASIC is a part, non-executive director of Scottish Hockey and member of the executive council of Scottish Student Sport.

The SRU has also forged partnerships with other government-funded agencies. For example, it lists the Food Standards Agency (FSA) and Cashback for Communities among its sponsors and partners.[2] The FSA promotes rugby to children in its healthy eating materials and through joint courses in 160 Scottish primary schools involving six weeks of rugby training. The SRU has received a sum of £1.4 million under Cashback for Communities – a programme that channels the proceeds of crime money into helping young people.[3] The scheme funds the Youth Coaching Course designed to prepare fifteen-to-nineteen-year-olds for voluntary coaching roles. According to the SRU, the course has led young people to take up the Scottish Vocational Qualification Community Coach Programme and helped development officers to recruit new volunteers to support their school and community initiatives.[4]

The links extend to the NHS. In 2008, Lothian Health Board gave the SRU £80,000 of scarce NHS funds to take rugby and health promotion into schools located in the most deprived areas of Edinburgh, mirroring Sport Scotland-funded rugby initiatives. What a horrible irony if an NHS programme may have exacerbated injury rates among less well-off children who already have much higher rates of injury and death than children in better-off areas. Rugby is being rolled out to children without proper thought of the risks to the young players, the majority of whom will never go on to play the game professionally but who may live a lifetime with the consequences of serious injury.[5]

The SRU also receives additional taxpayers' money through services that have now been privatised but which are in receipt of large sums of government funds. Group 4 (now G4S), the prison and security company which relies on public money for its business, and Scottish Hydro, once a publicly owned electricity company, both sponsored the SRU.

While all this money is going into supporting rugby union, the Scottish committee on the Child Safety Action Plans, a Europe-wide initiative, operates with no support and no resources. These ties can distort research priorities and the presentation of findings. It is an unscrutinised phenomenon, and yet as Dr Ken Quarrie, a leading researcher in the area, has warned, 'Not to declare [conflicts of interest] will indeed undermine the trust the public places in scientists and doctors as a professional group.'[6] Such conflicts of course extend to academics with close ties to the rugby unions, many of whom are in receipt of funds and deeply enmeshed in the sport.[7] Studies can be designed and interpreted to obscure the true risks.

This rugby-professional-academic-medical-business-government establishment rebuts the sport's public health critics with a set of familiar but flawed arguments. For example, public health advocates stand accused of discouraging sport to the neglect of the obesity problem. But any argument about the health benefits of increased sporting activity has to include measures which minimise the risk of injury. More than half the benefits of physical exercise may be lost through injuries, which can result in the abandonment of sport altogether.[8] Injured children cannot play, and this affects their educational attainment, their confidence and their fitness. But it does not have to be this way: Sweden has the lowest rates of injury and obesity and yet the highest levels of sports activity in Europe.[9]

Another argument of rugby advocates is that the injury rate is no worse than in other sports like skiing, trampolining, and horse riding. Even if this were the case, few of these sports take place on school premises, let alone as compulsory activities, so the duty of care falls to parents or other authorities. It is also difficult to compare injuries across sports because either data are not collected in a standardised way or not analysed. As we show in Part II, differences in injury definitions, methods of recording events, the experience of observers, and the use of protective equipment make it difficult to compare the frequency of injuries. There is also a lack of information on participation to link to the injury data. The truth is in many instances we just do not know what injury rates are across many sports except where special studies have been conducted. Eventing (an equestrian sport) and skiing are exceptions here. The exceptionally high injury rate in equestrianism has led the British Eventing governing body to take the issue very seriously, and it now records, publishes and monitors injuries by cause.[10]

Injury surveillance is not a new idea, nor are concerns about rugby. Editorials and papers on the issue date back decades with multiple authors and commentators calling for better surveillance and monitoring, especially of spinal injuries. Nonetheless, the proponents of rugby injury monitoring and advocates for improved safety are ignored, dismissed or subjected to ad hominem attacks. Recently one surgeon in Glasgow who had seen a number of serious injuries to professional rugby players received a lawyer's letter from the SRU when he expressed his concerns.

7

Impossible to Ignore

Following the removal of our website and publications in 2010, and the abrupt and untimely closure of the Centre for International Public Health Policy, I left the University of Edinburgh and moved down to London in 2011. The work on injuries in Scotland stopped, but the issue was kept alive by others: the independent member of the Scottish parliament (MSP) Margo MacDonald, chair of the health and sports committee, who had been a great ally, held a seminar on the matter in the Scottish Parliament. It is sad that she will never read this book, following her untimely death in April 2014. Scottish Nationalist Party MSP Ian McKee tabled parliamentary questions, and the Scottish Information Statistics Division started a pilot of injury data in some hospital A&E departments, which is still ongoing.

The SRU finds protection in ignorance. The axiom is: 'if we don't collect data we don't know the risks, and if we don't know the risks we don't need to act.' Lack of risk data is a handy tool in the contest with public health advocates.

The SRU will not know whether its rugby prevention strategies are working for the simple reason that there is no monitoring to evaluate them. As of today, despite repeated enquiries to the SRU and CMO, no proper surveillance is in place and there is anecdotal evidence that injury forms are still not being completed or returned. It is clear that this now professional sport is still overseen by an amateur governance system. The corporate checks and controls that should be in place are lacking. But this in itself does not explain the failure of public health bodies and ministers to intervene.

Injury rates from rugby are high indeed; unacceptably, every injury is a failure of care in the game. The question is: must we allow the commercial interests of universities and rugby unions to trump public health and the safety of children? The cost of implementing an injury surveillance system is paltry compared with the millions of pounds of sponsorship money and government funding spent on the sport. It is infinitely less than the suffering caused by the collective inaction of the public health community and the authorities.

The Winds of Change Are in the Air

In 2013 the expensive public school Glenalmond College, which has been a breeding ground for some of Scotland's most illustrious players, announced it would withdraw from a raft of fixtures for fear that the gulf in size between schoolboy players could lead to its pupils being injured. It based this decision on the 'degree of risk' to the first fifteen.[1] But change is not happening fast enough. In October

2013 I received a telephone call from a mother whose son, a brilliant musician who was shortlisted for the BBC Young Musician of the Year award, attends Haberdashers Aske School in England, a public fee paying school. The head teacher of the school had told the mother in writing that rugby was compulsory, no different from English or maths. In response to her concerns about injury she was told she was being overprotective. She had to remove her child from school, but how many children continue to play in fear of the game because parents find it difficult to stand up to authority?

In July 2013, former International Rugby Board medical advisor Dr Barry O'Driscoll, a former Ireland international and the uncle of rugby international player Brian O'Driscoll, resigned after fifteen years in service in protest over the sport's governing body revision to the assessment test used for concussion. He stated that the International Rugby Board was 'trivialising concussion' and described its five-minute test, the Pitch Side Concussion Assessment (PSCA), which can be requested by a player's team doctor and the match referee, as having 'no scientific, medical or rugby basis'. 'This experiment, which is employed by no other sport in the world, is returning the player to what is an extremely brutal arena.' 'The five-minute assessment of a player who has demonstrated distinct signs of concussion for 60 to 90 seconds, and usually longer, is totally discredited.'[2]

O'Driscoll said that the advice of the World Conference on Concussion in Sport, which has unanimously recommended that there should be no return to play on the same day of a suspected concussion, should stand.

'There is huge research and, unfortunately, it is showing that concussion is much more dangerous than we thought it was. Any cognitive or physical effect [should mean] you put a return to play off. Nobody in the world does a five-minute assessment apart from rugby.'

In his scathing interview to the *Scotsman* he said that 'the same player who eighteen months ago was given a minimum of seven days' recovery time is now given five minutes. There is no test that you can do in five minutes that will show that a player is not concussed. It is accepted the world over. We have all seen players who have appeared fine five minutes after a concussive injury then vomiting later in the night. To have this as acceptable in rugby, what kind of message are we sending out?'

'No sporting body in the world apart from the IRB have suggested that an athlete who has shown signs or symptoms of concussion can be cleared in five minutes,' O'Driscoll stressed. 'The IRB have refused to accept the significance of CTE, dementia, depression and suicide in NFL players with a history of concussion, as being in any way relevant to our game.'[3]

As we show in Part II, concussion is a leading cause of rugby injury among children too. If the IRB has such little regard for the welfare of valuable professional players then what hope is there for our children who have no economic value in the rugby market place?

In March 2014, the Labour MP Chris Bryant called for a parliamentary inquiry into concussion in sport, saying the RFU and other bodies were in 'complete denial' about the dangers, especially to young players.[4] Meanwhile, the *Mail on Sunday* is spearheading a campaign about rugby and concussion, led by rugby players themselves.[5] But we should not have to wait for professional players to win legal actions or settle for large sums out of court. The time for change is now. Any delay leaves children at serious risk of harm. Do we have to wait for the son of a senior politician to be seriously injured before change comes? Or for mothers to finally unite to force the collection and publication of data? Until such time as politicians, teachers and parents unite in the common cause of protecting children from unnecessary harm, then schoolchildren will have no advocates to protect them and to ensure that they can enjoy 'healthy minds in healthy bodies'.

Part II

Hospital Pass: Questions for Parents to Ask

Allyson M. Pollock
and Nikesh Parekh

Every parent has to decide whether the risks of school rugby are acceptable for their child. Good decisions must be based on evidence. We have surveyed all the relevant studies from across the world and gathered the information needed to answer some of the crucial questions that parents might want to ask when considering whether their child should play rugby.

Schools should be in a position to answer many of these questions. But seldom, if ever, do they inform, let alone consult, parents and children about the risks of injury from playing rugby. Rarely does a school monitor these risks or reveal what, if anything, it is doing to minimise them. Children are being exposed to considerable risk without being provided with information upon which they and their parents can base their consent, and without adequate support for the consequences of serious injuries.

Rugby is a high-impact collision sport that entails an expectation of some injuries. At what point do injuries become sufficiently serious and sufficiently frequent to be unacceptable? Deciding where this line should be drawn creates disagreement between those in the sporting establishment who wish to increase rugby's popularity and expand its commercial value, and those in the public health community who start from the position that most injuries are avoidable. Whichever way we choose to answer the question, it must be based on evidence.

1. What Is the Risk of Injury If a Child Plays Rugby?

As we highlighted in Part I, our study of rugby injuries in six Scottish schools suggests there is a 17 per cent (or about one in six) chance of a child getting seriously injured in a season of competitive school rugby, where 'serious' means at least one week's absence from sport is required to recover. However, in other studies of rugby injuries the probability of a child sustaining an injury in a season varies from 12 to 90 per cent (see Table 3). The trouble is that these studies differ widely in how they define and measure the risk of injury, and in how the data is collected.

The first problem is to define what counts as an injury. This is a big sticking point with much of the existing work that has been done. For example, the definition of a reportable youth rugby injury ranges from 'any physical complaint' caused by playing rugby, to an injury that prevents a player participating in the sport for at least one week.[1] These definitional vagaries distort injury estimates and undermine comparisons.

A good definition is crucial. It must be neither too narrow nor too broad; neither limited to the most severe injuries nor admitting every trivial complaint. But getting the balance right is a challenge. The definition of injury by the World Health Organisation is: 'The physical damage that results when a human body is suddenly subjected to energy in amounts that exceed the threshold of physiological tolerance.'[2] But this is too broad to be useful for a study of rugby injuries; it would include every knock, graze and bruise and there is little interest in preventing those.

In 2007, the International Rugby Board's Rugby Injury Consensus Group provided a definition of injury as 'any physical complaint, which was caused by a transfer of energy that exceeded the body's ability to maintain its structural and/or functional integrity, that was sustained by a player during a rugby match or rugby training, irrespective of the need for medical attention or time-loss from rugby activities. An injury that results in a player receiving medical attention is referred to as a "medical-attention" injury and an injury that results in a player being unable to take full part in future rugby training or match play as a "time-loss" injury.'[3]

However, most studies use definitions that measure the severity of injury in terms of time out from participation in sport. An injury may only be recorded if it prevents the player from taking part in the next match or training session. The problem with such 'time-loss' definitions is that they produce significant bias and can result in many important injuries being left unrecorded.[4] While one player may decide not to participate in a future session of play because subjectively they rate their injury as severe, another player might choose to take part despite an objectively more serious complaint.

To get around this, a study of rugby union injuries in schoolboys in New Zealand defined an injury as 'any physical complaint caused by rugby during school training and matches', and justified this broad approach by pointing to eleven fractures that would not have been recorded using a time-loss definition, because the players did not take time out from the sport.[5] Unsurprisingly, this study recorded the highest injury rate out of all the epidemiological studies of school rugby injuries that we reviewed. The risk of injury was about 90 per cent over the course of a fifteen-match season, but if the definition were changed to encompass only those injuries that result in a one week absence from participation the risk would drop to between 12 and 30 per cent.[6]

Ultimately then, our review of worldwide epidemiological studies into the incidence of injury from youth rugby union shows no consistency in reported rates. There is almost a nineteen-fold difference between the highest and lowest reported incidence of injury, with the highest rate at 130 injuries per 1,000 player-hours and the lowest at seven injuries per 1,000 player-hours.

Despite the problems that come with a sole focus on time-loss, our own study of rugby union injuries in Scottish schools used the IRB's recommended definition. Its Rugby Injury Consensus Group also set out how the severity of an injury could be categorised by the amount of time away from the sport, specifically the 'number of days that have elapsed from the date of injury to the date of the player's return to full participation in team training and availability for match selection'.[7] Injuries could be regarded as: slight (0–1 days); minimal (2–3 days); mild (4–7 days); moderate (8–28 days); severe (more than 28 days); career-ending; and non-fatal catastrophic.[8]

A second issue when trying to compare study findings is variation in the way that injury is measured. Not all players play every game, or even whole games. They may only play for part of the season, or be injured half way through. If substitutes are included in the data it will take in players who are not being exposed to as much risk. To get around this, epidemiologists have tried to calculate the true exposure to risk using the total number of player-hours on the pitch, rather than the total number of players on the field or in the squad. Most studies of sporting injury use a variant of this method, measuring the injury incidence rate per player-exposure, giving a result of 'x' number of injuries per 1,000 player-hours.

But this is just not helpful for most people. What are we to make of risk when we are told that the rate of injury is two injuries per 1,000 player hours? None of us can know whether this is a high or a low risk. It is not only unfamiliar to a public audience but is also impossible to interpret at the level of the individual and is open to misinterpretation as people might be tempted to think that it means the risk of injury is two in a thousand games or two in a thousand players. Its only merit is to make comparisons across studies, but that is of no real help to parents.[30]

Expressing the risk of getting injured as a percentage or a proportion is readily grasped by everyone. It is the common way of understanding risk.[31] For example, compare the way risks are expressed for rugby and occupational injuries. Both activities involve a mathematical risk of injury that increases with the amount of exposure to the activity – the more time spent in a dangerous work environment or playing rugby, the more likely an injury becomes. So it is difficult to understand why the risks of injury from sport are not presented as probabilities, when workplace injuries are. Occupational injury statistics are translated for the public using probability theory. The UK Health and Safety Executive defines acceptable and unacceptable levels of occupational risk in terms of the probability that a serious adverse event will occur in one year, and not in terms of injury incidence rates per worker-exposure.[32] Similarly, the US National Safety Council produced an 'odds' table in

Table 3 Studies by author and year of publication, number of players, number of match injuries, exposure, injury incidence and converted to average probability of injury to a player in a typical season

Author and year of publication	Number of players	Number of injuries	Total exposure	Incidence of injury (95% confidence interval where given)	Average probability of injury to a player in a typical season*
Davidson 1978[9]	659	556	40,588 player-hours	13.7 injuries per 1,000 player-hours	21%
Davidson 1987[10]	Not given	1,444	82,107 player-hours	17.6 injuries per 1,000 player-hours	27%
Durie 2000[11]	442	189	6,880 player-hours	27.5 injuries per 1,000 player-hours	38%
Fuller 2011[12]	941	190	3,320 player-hours	57.2 (49.6, 66.0) injuries per 1,000 player-hours	63%
Gabbett 2008[13]	80	62	1,092 player-hours	56.8 (42.6, 70.9) injuries per 1,000 player-hours	63%
Haseler 2010[14]	210	39	1,636 player-hours	24 injuries per 1,000 player-hours	34%
Junge 2004[15]	123	225	1,734 player-hours†	129.8 injuries per 1,000 player-hours	90%
McIntosh 2010[16]	3,277	Game injuries: 1,841 Missed game injuries: 604	28,902 player-hours	Game injury: 63.7 (60.9, 66.7) injuries per 1,000 player-hours Missed game injury: 20.9 (19.3, 22.6) injuries per 1,000 player-hours	Game injury: 67% Missed game injury: 31%
Nathan 1983[17]	Not given	50	6,075 player-hours	8.2 injuries per 1,000 player-hours	13%
Nicol 2011[18]	470‡	26	2,406 player-hours	10.8 injuries per 1,000 player-hours	17%

Study					
Palmer-Green 2013[19]	School: 222 Academy: 250	School: 134 Academy: 109	School: 3,843 player-hours Academy: 2,343 player-hours	School: 35 injuries per 1,000 player-hours Academy: 47 injuries per 1,000 player-hours	School: 46% Academy: 56%
Pringle 1998[20]	Rugby union: 1,932 Rugby league: 1,730	Rugby union: 24 Rugby league: 36	Rugby union: 1,548 player-hours† Rugby league: 1,469 player-hours†	Rugby union: 15.5 injuries per 1000 player-hours Rugby league: 24.5 injuries per 1,000 player-hours	Rugby union: 24% Rugby league: 35%
Roux 1987[21]	Not given	353	5,0126 player-hours†	7.0 injuries per 1,000 player-hours	12%
Sparks 1985[22]	2,427‡	560	22,776 player-hours†	24.6 injuries per 1,000 player-hours†	35%
Bird 1998[23]	141	Not given	Not given	21.7 injuries per 100 player-games	Not measurable
Collins 2008[24]	Not given	488	32,014 match-exposures	15.2 injuries per 1,000 match-exposures	Not applicable
Marshall 2001[25]	Not given	12 concussions	1,071 player-games†	11.1 (4.8, 17.4) concussions per 1,000 player-games	Not applicable
Usman 2013[26]	Not given	Not given	Not given	10.7 (9.9, 11.6) upper limb injuries per 1,000 athletic-exposures	Not applicable
Garraway 2000[27]	251	Not given	Not given	Period prevalence 27.6 per 1,000 player-hours	Not applicable
Lee 1996[28]	1,705	148	1,829 player-seasons†	80.9 (68.0, 93.9) injuries per 1,000 player-seasons	Not applicable

* Average probability of injury to a player using the Poisson distribution model of Parekh et al.,[29] assuming a player plays a whole season of fifteen games with each game seventy minutes in duration as per under-nineteen IRB regulations. Injury incidence needs to be given as per 1,000 player-hours.

† Calculated post-hoc from figures in paper

‡ Matches and training combined, separate figures not available

response to frequent inquiries from people asking for the chances of a serious adverse event happening to them in particular situations. Meanwhile, the Statistical Office of the European Union (Eurostat) publishes information on injuries at work in terms of the 'number of accidents per 100,000 people'.

Take the example of a doctor discussing with a patient the possibility of complications during surgery. The patient will be told that there is an 'x' per cent chance of a particular complication occurring. Of course all patients have features that will alter their risk profile, just as children have different physiques that will affect the likelihood of them being injured, but patients still appreciate being given an average probability that a complication will occur.[33]

What parents want to know is the likelihood of their child being injured. Imagine as a parent you were told that over the course of a season, the average risk of serious injury to a player is 17 per cent, or one in six, and that in some schools it is as high as 33 per cent, or one in three. The decision to allow your child to play might alter, especially when coupled with information on the nature and severity of injuries and their long-term consequences. It might also change your attitude to injury insurance cover, particularly if you are advised to indemnify your own children against the risk of non-catastrophic injury.[34]

One might expect that authorities with a duty of care would ensure that a methodology is provided to present sports injury risk as an average probability that also incorporates the player time-exposure within the statistic. But they have not. Nor is one provided in the literature. So we approached Professor Stewart Hodges from the Cass Business School who, with some ingenuity, found a statistical method that allowed us to convert player-exposure into a probability of risk.

The following paragraphs explain how we transformed our raw study data into a 17 per cent probability of injury. They are technical, and non-mathematicians may choose to skip them and turn to page 97.

When schoolboy rugby injuries are reported using injury incidence rates – 'x' injuries per 1,000 player-hours – the denominator is calculated as follows:

> Number of players (fifteen playing at one time in a rugby team) x Number of matches in a school season x Length of one match (up to seventy minutes at school level)

This calculation gives us the total 'player-hours' in a season and is usually scaled up to 1,000. Our study of six Scottish schools reported a match injury incidence of 10.8 injuries per 1,000 player hours. We recorded thirty-seven injuries in half a school rugby season, of which just over half required A&E attendance. Over 60 per cent of the injuries prevented the student from taking further part in any rugby for at least three weeks, while over 20 per cent caused students to take time off school. Our study did not observe injuries in the first half of the rugby season, which tends to be more dangerous, and ours was therefore an underestimate of the overall injury rate. A subsequent study of youth rugby union injuries in the UK involving schoolchildren from the under-9s to the under-17s over a whole season, using a similar injury definition to ours, reported an overall injury rate of twenty-four injuries per 1,000 player-hours.[35]

These incidence rates can be transformed into a probability of injury over a stated period of time using a model based on the Poisson distribution. The Poisson distribution is a way of modelling probability, developed by the great French mathematician Siméon Denis Poisson in the nineteenth century. Broadly speaking, the Poisson distribution can be used as a predictive model for the probability of injury to a particular player (or set of players) in the course of playing a season's rugby matches, and it is equally applicable to other sports. This statistical model provides the most natural framework in which to understand the prevalence of injuries both across players and over time. The Poisson distribution forms the basis of most standard models in risk analysis. In fact, one of its first applications was to assess the risk of injuries to soldiers within the Prussian cavalry. It is perhaps worth noting that although the Poisson distribution is sometimes called 'the law of rare events', it requires not that events be rare, but that the time to the next event is independent of the time since the last one. Such a model is justified in sports injuries provided it is reasonable to assume that injuries occur with a known average rate and independently of the time since the last injury. The model therefore requires that players who sustain an injury recover before returning to play. If sporting bodies and schools are ensuring that players are properly rehabilitated, as any parent would expect, then this model is very useful in sports injury risk analysis.

The model's main input is the incidence rate as number of injuries per player-hour. The Poisson distribution then predicts the probabilities of the different possible numbers of injuries resulting from a particular time-exposure.[36] Using this method, the injury incidence that we recorded in our own small study – 10.8 injuries per 1,000 player-hours – can be expressed as the average school player having a 17 per cent chance of getting injured in a season of competitive rugby. Both approaches use the same injury data to present risk in different ways.

Applying the same method to the data collected by other studies is also possible. The last column of Table 3 displays the results of using the Poisson distribution to transform injury incidence rates reported in several studies into average risk probabilities for a season of fifteen matches. The probabilities are based on an assumption of an average school player completing fifteen matches, which is a number consistent with existing studies.[37] When it is expressed as 'x' injuries per 1,000 player-hours, the injury incidence rate could give the impression that the chance of injury to a player is generally very low. But when we look at the probabilities of injury we can see that even in the study with the very lowest reported injury incidence rate, the chance of a child sustaining an injury that requires at least a week's absence from the sport is still a significant 12 per cent.[38]

If we consider injuries that do not cause absence, but may still require medical treatment, then the risks are substantially greater. One can appreciate from Table 3 how critical the injury definition is to the injury incidence rate and the probability of injury to a player. If all injuries experienced by a school rugby team are included, then the probability of injury to the average player over the course of a season may be up to 90 per cent. It is also clear from the data that the likelihood of injury increases with age.

We hope and recommend that the model we have outlined becomes the standard way to present sports injury data. Communicating risk to parents and children in a manner they can understand is essential if they are to make informed decisions about which sports to play. Research has shown that people are willing to accept risks that are 1,000 times greater when those risks are taken on voluntarily (such as a bungee jump) rather than without consent.[39] But without sufficient information, schoolchildren playing competitive rugby do not give *informed* consent to the risks of serious injury, and nor do their parents or guardians.

2. How Does the Risk of Injury in Rugby Compare with Other Sports?

A systematic review of worldwide sports injury studies to quantify risk in children under the age of sixteen showed that rugby and ice hockey were the most injury-prone team sports.[40] These data, in combination with other studies comparing sports in youth populations, suggests that rugby carries the highest risk of injury among competitive sports commonly played in UK schools.[41]

This is reflected in research that focuses on hospital A&E departments. At one A&E in Northern Ireland, upon which a study was published in 2003, 43 per cent of eleven-to-eighteen-year-olds who attended casualty with a sports injury had sustained it playing rugby, three times more than from football or hockey.[42] Similarly, at the main A&E

department in Cardiff, Wales, rugby contributed to the greatest number of sports injury presentations, accounting for 25 per cent of all injuries.[43] Of course, the injuries seen in A&E are only the tip of the iceberg. Many more complaints are dealt with at school or by a GP.

The vast majority of the injuries presented at A&E were to boys. For girls, netball accounted for the largest number of injuries resulting in a visit to casualty, but as rugby is becoming increasingly popular among females the number of rugby injuries has risen. There is an urgent need for good research on schoolgirl rugby to establish if the risks are equivalent to those faced by boys. Overall, the number of sport injuries treated at A&E has been rising steadily over the past few years.[44]

A different location for studying the relative risks of injury is at school itself. In New Zealand, a doctor visited a school over one season to compare the injuries of fourteen-to-eighteen-year-old schoolboys in ten school rugby teams and twelve school football teams.[45] The incidence of injury was almost three times higher in rugby union compared with football. There was approximately a five times higher risk of concussion or dislocation, and almost a seven times higher risk of fracture from playing rugby. In the course of the study, three rugby players had their season ended by the severity of their injuries, two with shoulder dislocations and one with a torn knee ligament. No football players sustained such severe injuries.

Another study compared catastrophic injury, defined by the IRB as 'brain or spinal cord injury that results in permanent (>12 months) severe functional disability', between various collision sports and activities. The risk of catastrophic injury in rugby union was calculated at 0.8 per 100,000 exposed population per year in England and 0.9 per 100,000 injuries per year in Ireland.[46] There is a lower risk of catastrophic injury in rugby union than in rugby league, American football and ice hockey. It is important to note that cognitive disability (diminished brain function) was not included despite good evidence for the negative long-term impacts of repeated concussions.

Britain's Health and Safety Executive (HSE) has had little involvement in the publication of sports injury data. Although the HSE seeks to reduce risks to 'as low as is reasonably practicable', it is not currently doing so in the case of rugby.[47] Many catastrophic spinal injuries are preventable and it is this fact that in our opinion makes the risk unacceptable.[48]

There is a culture of expectation and acceptance of school rugby injuries in comparison with other sports in the UK. It seems that the main reasons for this are the contact nature of the sport and its traditional association with masculinity.[49] It is not uncommon for a broken nose, for example, to be looked upon as a something of a badge of honour among players. Such attitudes are seen across the game. A study of rugby players in a British university identified a deep-rooted and socially valued 'culture of risk' that leads them to continue playing through pain and injury for the good of the team and to demonstrate their masculinity. The study found a range of understandings among players of what constitutes an injury – some believed it was the physical inability to play, rather than merely pain.[50] But these players are adhering to a culture of risk without truly knowing what the risk is. A radical cultural change that embraces the well-being of all participants is needed within the sport, championed by the government, the IRB and the international players who act as role models.

Unfortunately rugby union has become more dangerous since it became a professional sport in 1995. Changes to the rules to create more open play with fewer stoppages have coincided with a doubling of injury risk at both junior and professional level.[51] The England Rugby Injury Surveillance Project reported that in professional rugby union there were 655 match injuries in total in the 2011–12 season (plus another 323 in training – a third of all injuries), down from 746 the previous year although the number has fluctuated over the nine years of data collection between a minimum of 482 in 2005–06 and a maximum of 755 in 2006–07. But worryingly there has been a trend towards more severe injuries since 2002–03, measured by average time away from play, particularly among the most serious injuries requiring three-to-six-month absences.[52]

3. What Kinds of Injury Are Common?

The most common injury types are basic grazes, cuts and bruises from knocks that occur in the contact phases of the game. These are straightforward to manage, are unlikely to require any medical attention and have no significant physical consequences for a player. These injuries fall under 'slight' on the scale of severity and are not generally recorded, although they may, of course, engender fear, discomfort and pain in the child.

Injuries that are usually recorded range from the frequent and relatively minor – such as muscle and ligament

Most common injuries requiring medical help

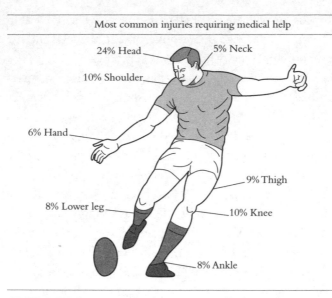

24% Head

5% Neck

10% Shoulder

6% Hand

9% Thigh

8% Lower leg

10% Knee

8% Ankle

CRISP: RFU Community Rugby Injury Surveillance Project – Seasonal Report 2011-12, *available at*: http://www.bath.ac.uk/health/projects/rfu-rugbyinjury/documents/CRISP_Season_Report_1112.pdf

sprains – to the rare and catastrophic – such as major injuries to the brain and spine causing life-long disability or even death. Some injuries are both common and serious, including concussions, fractures, tendon and ligament ruptures and shoulder and other joint dislocations. Bone fractures account for 18 to 27 per cent of all youth rugby injuries and are most commonly of the finger, wrist, clavicle (a shoulder bone) or nose. In our review of the literature, the most frequently reported types of injury were concussions, fractures, sprains, strains, dislocations and subluxations (see Table 4). Concussion was reported by nineteen studies and ranged from 2.2 to 24.6 per cent of all injuries recorded. Ligament injuries, sprains and strains

Table 4 Nature of injury sustained and highest and lowest percentage of all injuries in each category and number of studies providing data

Injury	Percentage of all injuries in each category (highest and lowest)	Number of studies*
Fracture	3–27%	14
Ligament injuries, sprains and strains	15.7–46.7%	10
Dislocation and subluxation	0.5–10.8%	10
Laceration, contusion and haematoma	2.7–46.0%	12
Concussion	2.2–24.6%	19

* Data provided by twenty-one studies[53]

combined were reported in ten studies and ranged from 15.7 to 46.7 per cent of all injuries recorded. Fractures were reported in fourteen studies and ranged from 3 to 27 per cent of all reported injuries, while laceration, contusion and haematoma combined were reported in twelve studies and ranged from 2.7 to 46 per cent of all injuries recorded. Finally, 0.5 to 10.8 per cent of all injuries were dislocations and subluxations. Dislocations most commonly affect the shoulder and, along with other shoulder injuries (to the joint or supporting tissues), have a disproportionate impact often requiring long-term absence from sport.[54]

Rugby injuries may harm any part of the body, but the neck and head area and the upper and lower limbs are most vulnerable, while the trunk is less often injured. The majority of studies show the head, face, and neck to be most frequently injured areas, contributing on average 30 per cent of total injuries.[55] Of team sports, only American football, ice hockey and lacrosse are more hazardous to the head and neck than rugby.[56] Some studies have shown the lower limbs of younger players sustain the most injuries, which tallies with experience from senior and professional rugby.[57] In the youth game, the shoulder, knee and ankle are very common sites of injury.[58]

4. What Is Concussion and What Effects Can It Have on a Child's Long-Term Health and Academic Progress?

Concussion results when the brain is shaken following either a direct or indirect blow to the head.[59] At a cellular level, this triggers a 'neurometabolic cascade' of ionic, metabolic and pathophysiological events accompanied by microscopic axonal injury.[60] Symptoms of concussion include headache, dizziness and sleep disturbance with loss of consciousness occurring in about 10 per cent of cases.[61] These symptoms usually resolve within seven to ten days, although they may last longer for children and adolescents.[62] In about 10–20 per cent of concussions, symptoms can endure for weeks, months or even years, leading to a classification of post-concussion syndrome (PCS).[63]

What are the immediate and short-term effects of concussion?

A meta-analysis of studies which compared athletes who sustained a concussion during sport with non-concussed control groups or comparisons with pre-season baseline measures demonstrated significant deterioration in neurocognitive function (such as information processing, planning and memory abilities), self-report symptoms (somatic, cognitive and neuropsychological) and postural control both immediately following a concussion and up to fourteen days after the injury.[64]

What are the long-term effects of concussion and repeat concussions?

A large study in Denmark among hospital admissions of less than two days for concussion found a significantly higher rate of cognitive dysfunction among patients with a history of two concussions compared to those on their first admission to hospital for concussion.[65] This may mean repeat concussions cause a deterioration in cognitive function or that lower cognitive ability is a risk factor for concussion.[66]

Studies of the effects of multiple concussions suffer from methodological shortcomings. However, there is accumulative evidence of an association between multiple concussions and a worsening of cognitive function.[67]

Adult rugby union players in Australia with a history of three or more concussions have been found to have significantly reduced mental processing speed compared to players with no concussion history.[68] In the USA, athletes with a history of two or more concussions performed significantly worse on measures of attention, concentration and academic performance than athletes with no concussion history or a history of only one concussion.[69]

Cognitive deficits have been found in sportspeople who have engaged professionally in contact sports, even after retirement. A large survey of 2,552 retired American

National Football League (NFL) players in 2005 compared players with a history of concussion to those without
and found a higher than expected prevalence of late-life
memory problems and mild cognitive impairment among
those with a history of concussion, which appeared to
worsen significantly with an increase of the number of concussions sustained during a players' career.[70] Studies from
Canada have also demonstrated an association between a
history of concussion among former university American
football and ice hockey players and poorer memory and
verbal fluency, as well as electrophysiological abnormalities on testing thirty years later compared to athletes with
no history of concussion.[71]

Physiology

There is evidence of acute and non-acute electrophysiological changes in the brains of concussed patients.[72] Grey
matter abnormalities have been found four months after
an episode of mild traumatic brain injury (TBI) (a term
often used synonymously with concussion).[73] Even below
the threshold for concussion there is evidence of disruption of the blood–brain barrier indicated by elevated levels
of brain protein S100B in the blood samples of affected
American football players who experienced 'sub-concus-
sive head hits', but with no such finding among players
who had not experienced such trauma.[74] This raises the
possibility that the later cognitive decline found among
players of contact sports with a history of repeated head
trauma could be linked to the antibodies formed due to
the presence of the S100B protein leaking back across

into the brain the next time the blood–brain barrier is opened up.[75]

There may also be long-term physical damage to the brain as a result of repeat concussions in contact sports, although current evidence for this is based on autopsy case reports, which may suffer from selection bias.[76] Although the effects of anabolic steroid use have not been ruled out, the possibility of a causal link is strong (REF 77 C+D). Chronic traumatic encephalopathy (CTE), a neurodegenerative disease associated with repetitive brain trauma and only diagnosable on autopsy, has been found in former boxers, American footballers, hockey players and wrestlers and recently for the first time in a rugby player in Scotland.[77] CTE was initially known as dementia pugilistica or 'punch drunk' syndrome, where boxers whose fighting style led to frequent blows to the head developed motor deficits and mental confusion, similar but neuropathologically distinct from other neurodegenerative disorders.[78] In 2005, a significantly higher prevalence of early onset Alzheimer's disease was found in the NFL players surveyed than among the general USA male population.[79] A systematic review of the literature has also found a strong association between moderate and severe TBI and the development of dementia of the Alzheimer's type, but only a suggestion of an association with mild TBI and this was only where a loss of consciousness had been established.[80] A meta-analysis of head injury has found a significant increase of 57 per cent in developing Parkinson's disease among people with a history of head trauma resulting in concussion and loss of consciousness.[81]

Risk factors for concussion

The structural and physiological differences in the developing brains of children compared to the fully developed adult brain requires different approaches to diagnosis, recovery assessment and the management of concussion.[82] Children take longer to recover and are at increased risk of catastrophic injuries such as second-impact syndrome, where a player sustains a second concussion without fully recovering from the first, possibly leading to diffuse cerebral swelling and death.[83] In a study of emergency department attendees in the US between 1978 and 2004, concussion was found to be more prevalent among rugby players under the age of eighteen than it was for adult rugby players.[84] With respect to recovery, another American study found that thirteen-to-sixteen-year-olds took around two days longer, on average, to return to normal levels on measures of memory, reaction speed and postconcussive symptoms than eighteen-to-twenty-two-year-olds; seven or eight days depending on the measure against five or six days respectively.[85]

Gender is a risk factor with female athletes at a higher risk of concussion, likely to report more symptoms and to take longer to recover than males.[86] Also the likelihood of sustaining a concussion is increased when a player has sustained a concussion in the past.[87]

Diagnosing concussion

Sports concussions that do not involve loss of consciousness or convulsions can be difficult to diagnose – athletes may inaccurately report symptoms or they may withhold information in order to continue playing.[88] The diagnosis and management of concussion includes comprehensive neuropsychological testing and postural tests.[89] The use of multiple evaluation tools may be most effective in correctly diagnosing concussion although there is a lack of evidence to support exactly which combination of symptom scales, checklists, balance testing and neurocognitive testing to use.[90]

There is an absence of objective tests to diagnose concussion and the brain damage that may result, although this is an area of active research for new biomarkers and magnetic resonance imaging techniques.[91] Standard computerised tomography (CT) or magnetic resonance imaging (MRI) scans are used to rule out more serious head injury.[92]

Recommended tools to assist the clinical assessment of concussion on the sports field include the Sports Concussion Assessment Tool version 3 (SCAT3), the Child SCAT3 card (for five-to-twelve-year-olds) and the Concussion Recognition Tool, all developed from the Fourth International Conference on Concussion in Sport held in Zurich, Switzerland in November 2012, known as the Zurich Consensus Statement on Concussion in Sport 2012.[93] The SCAT3 and the Child SCAT3 are designed for clinicians, while non-medical personnel can use the Concussion Recognition Tool. However, the SCAT tools lack any measure of reliability, sensitivity or specificity. Although developed by a panel of experts from published sources, thus establishing face and content validity, similar to most concussion scales they were not empirically developed prior to clinical use.[94]

Second-impact syndrome

Second-impact (or double-impact) syndrome can occur in
sport when a player sustains a second brain trauma before
recovering fully from a prior concussion or other serious
brain injury.[95] The second knock can occur minutes, days
or weeks after the first and can be quite minor. It is thought
that the second trauma leads to a disruption of the normal
regulation of blood flow resulting in diffuse swelling of
the brain, raising the pressure within the skull and causing
the brainstem – which is critical to a human's ability to
breathe – to get squashed.[96] It is extremely serious, possibly
permanently disabling or fatal. It is associated with a high
mortality rate.[97]

The existence of the phenomenon is disputed but incidents have been reported in American football, boxing and
ice hockey. One study reported seventeen cases among
young adults twenty-one years or younger in the US over
a thirty-year period.[98] The young are more susceptible to
second-impact syndrome than adults but the mechanism
behind this is not fully understood. Although the syndrome is not a common event, every effort must be made to
ensure that no athlete, playing rugby or any other contact
sport, suffers this catastrophic condition.

5. How Much Time Do Injured Children Lose from School and Sport?

In our review, we identified fourteen studies which used
a 'time-loss' injury definition, with eight of those providing detailed data on the severity of injury, which

is defined as a certain number of days absent from the game.

Moderate injuries (which required a player to be absent from playing for eight to twenty-eight days) ranged from 21.1 to 68 per cent, while severe injuries (which required a player to be absent from playing for more than twenty-eight days) ranged from 5.8 to 32 per cent. One study reported that injured players in school had an average (mean) absence from playing of twenty-seven days compared to thirty-three days for elite youth players at English Premiership Academies.[104] In our study, 13.5 per cent of players were absent from playing rugby for more than eighty-four days after being injured.[105] Again, our study found eight (21.6 per cent) of the children injured required time off school with three requiring more than three days

Table 5 For each study by author and year, number and percentage of injuries by severity of injury – minimal, mild, moderate, severe (defined as number of days absent from playing)

	Minimal (2–3d)	Mild (4–7d)	Moderate (8–28d)	Severe (>28d)	Not specified
Fuller 2011[99]	54 (28.4%)	45 (23.7%)	40 (21.1%)	41 (21.6%)	10 (5.3%)
Haseler 2010[100]	16 (41%)		16 (41%)	7 (18%)	Not available
Usman 2013[101]			412 (68%)	194 (32%)	Not available
	0d	1–7d	8–28d	>28d	
Sparks 1985[102]	19 (2.5%)	421 (54.5%)	287 (37.2%)	45 (5.8%)	
	<1 week	1–2 weeks	3–6 weeks	7–12 weeks	>12 weeks
Nicol 2011[103]	6 (16.2%)	7 (18.9%)	17 (45.9%)	2 (5.4%)	5 (13.5%)

away, including the one child with spinal injuries who was away from school long-term.[106]

Other research found twenty-three schoolboys (16 per cent of their cohort) required time away from school as a result of rugby injury with, on average, 2.2 days of schooling missed. Fractures alone accounted for an average of 5.5 days of missed schooling.[107]

6. What Phase of Play Is Most Dangerous?

Various phases of the game of rugby union, such as the tackle, scrum, ruck and maul, involve collisions and the use of force. Tackles are responsible for the highest percentage of injuries to junior rugby players, while the less common scrum is proportionately more dangerous.

In our review of all studies in children and adolescents aged under twenty-one we found that the tackle, which includes both tackling and being tackled, accounted for the majority of injuries, with two studies stating that almost half of all injuries were sustained because of tackles (39.6 to 64 per cent). Being tackled was generally found to account for more injuries (19.4 to 65 per cent) than active tackling (18.5 to 40 per cent). Ruck and maul accounted for the third highest rates of injuries (8.3 to 31.5 per cent) after tackling and being tackled. With one exception, scrums accounted for the fourth highest rates (2 to 36 per cent).

Tackles account for between 47–60 per cent of recorded injuries. The average severity of these injuries requires one month's absence from further participation in sport.[109] In a large research study of tackle injuries conducted on seventy-one rugby clubs across 964 matches in Scotland,

Table 6 By phase of play, percentage of injuries (highest and lowest percentage recorded in each study) and number of studies

Phase of play	Range – highest and lowest percentage of injuries recorded	Number of studies reporting percentage injury
All tackle	39.6–64%	10
– Active tackle	18.5–40%	9
– Recipient of tackle	19.4–40.5%	9
Scrum	2–18%	9
Ruck and Maul	15–31.5%	5

Sources:[108]

30 per cent of injuries were lower limb sprains, strains and ligament ruptures, while 16 per cent were shoulder dislocations and 12 per cent concussions.[110] An Australian study of thirty-three schools categorised injury types by those that occurred while tackling and those that occurred while being tackled. The most common injuries in both cases were sprains of the ligaments at joints (approximately 20 to 25 per cent) and fractures (also approximately 20 to 25 per cent).[111]

Both the tackler and tackled player sustain injuries. The incidence of these injuries is about basic physics. The injury is related to the force with which a player commits to the tackle or conversely the force with which the player holding the ball is moving. It is a question of player mass and player acceleration. The player with a lower momentum is injured 80 per cent of the time when tackle injuries occur.[112]

Efforts have been made to address the risks of serious injuries by outlawing high tackles (tackles above the shoulders) and spear tackles (tackles where players are lifted off the ground and driven headfirst into the ground). These are steps in the right direction, but another important area where injury prevention should be focussed is the tackle going in behind the tackled player's line of vision at speed, which is associated with a high risk of injury.[113]

Attitudes towards tackling and safety have been researched in detail in South Africa, where players from nine schools completed a questionnaire. When asked 'What is important to you when making a tackle?' the top ranked answer was 'Bringing down the ball-carrier at all costs', while the bottom ranked answer of eleven alternatives was 'Safety of the ball-carrier'.[114] This attitude is highly concerning and should not be blamed on the players but rather the culture of the game that they see on television, grow-up with and train under.

Although the tackle phase of play is associated with a far greater number of injuries than the scrum, the propensity for the tackle to cause injury has been rated as 'average' in contrast to the 'high' rating given to the scrum. It has been estimated that scrums carry a 60 per cent greater risk of injury than tackles.[115] Consequently the scrum has come under the greatest scrutiny with high levels of medical concern for the past forty years.[116] Most studies have found the scrum to contribute to less than 15 per cent of the total number of injuries recorded but this is because scrums occur far less frequently than tackles.[117]

The scrum has traditionally been associated with severe spinal injuries and still carries the highest risk of disabling injury.[118] The cervical spine, the part of the spine that runs down the neck, is especially vulnerable to the scrum and other head-first collisions seen in rugby.[119] When the neck is bent forwards, as in the engagement of a scrum, the cervical spine straightens which means that any force to the head is transmitted directly down the spine and very little shock is absorbed by the surrounding neck muscles. If the force exceeds the strength of the vertebrae (the bones of the spine that protect the spinal cord and nervous system) they compress upon one another leading to a broken neck. Following the compression and break, if any of the bones are pushed into an abnormal alignment impinging the spinal cord then paralysis can be the consequence.[120] Excessive forward-bending (hyperflexion) of the neck, with or without rotation, can also cause spinal cord damage.[121]

In the last decade the IRB has introduced regulations for under-19 players to reduce the duration and amount of force that the engagement of the scrum inflicts upon the front-row. However, a study published in 2008 found that front-row forwards were experiencing significantly more neck injuries than players in any other position. Either regulations were insufficient or they were not being properly enforced; most likely it was a combination of the two.

Furthermore, an audit of serious neck injuries requiring admission to specialist spinal hospital units among under-19 rugby union players in Great Britain and Ireland from 1996–2010 found that serious neck injuries were continuing 'with a low but persistent frequency'.[122] Although the tackle contributed to more of these neck injuries than the scrum (seventeen as against thirteen out of thirty-six injuries recorded), spinal cord injury was significantly more common as a result of the scrum and it is these that lead to permanent disability.[123]

Further evidence of the extremely high levels of compression force generated on engagement of the scrum has been found in a 2013 study conducted by researchers at the University of Bath and the English RFU. They likened the speed at which the front-row engaged in the scrum to that of 'an athletic sprinter leaving the blocks'. The combined weight of the school scrum (eight forwards) was just less than 700 kilograms. As force is the product of mass and acceleration, it is easy to see how dangerously large forces are generated.[124] The study showed a peak compression force of 9,100 Newtons, which is equivalent to the force of being hit by a 14,500 kilogram double-decker bus accelerating at 0.6 metres per second squared. This kind of force can cause catastrophic injuries and can also lead to long-term damage of the spine and chronic back pain.[125]

Given all this evidence, new efforts are being made to reduce the risk of scrum injuries with an amendment to the rules. From 2013 the IRB trialled a new scrum engagement sequence of 'crouch-bind-set' instead of the previous 'crouch-touch-engage'. It is hoped that the forces transmitted upon the engagement of the front-row forwards will be cut by 25 per cent by the new routine, reducing the risk of disabling neck and spine injuries and lessening the chances of the scrum collapsing. We eagerly await the urgent evaluation of this change to scrummaging. Much more also needs to be done in respect of the tackle.

7. Which Is the Most Dangerous Position to Play In?

The most serious rugby injuries – those to the neck and cervical spine – occur most frequently to the front-row forwards and in particular to the hooker.[126] The risk of injury of different player positions at school level is summarised in Table 7.[127] Rather than analysing individual positions, some studies have tended to consider how the rate of injuries compares between the two distinct roles for players: forwards and backs. This is a reasonable approach with only forwards taking part in certain aspects of the game, like the scrum, and backs more involved in open play. At junior level, front-row forwards are at the greatest risk of neck injuries.[128] The risk of sustaining an injury to the cervical spine is also reported to be highest among front-row forwards in both professional and school rugby.[129] There is however no difference between forwards and backs in risks of injury overall as Table 7 shows.

Between 2008 and 2011 in South Africa, nineteen potentially life-threatening or permanently debilitating spinal cord injuries were recorded at schoolboy level among just under 530,000 school players.[131] The same study found that overall, including injuries from the senior game (which saw twenty-six spinal injuries over the period), hookers suffered 46 per cent of permanently disabling injuries, of which 83 per cent came from the scrum. No backs suffered a spinal injury that resulted in permanent disability.

The vulnerability of the hooker is hardly surprising. The physique of a hooker is generally smaller than the

Table 7 Percentage of all injuries (range – highest and lowest percentage recorded) by position of play in seven studies

Position of play (alternative names)		Percentage of all injuries attributable*
Forwards	All forwards	43.8–56.3%
	Loose head prop and tight head prop	2.1–14.5%
	Hooker	7.4–31.6%
	Looks (second rows)	4.2–12.6%
	Blindside flanker and openside flanker	5.8–14.7%
	Number eight	6.8–17.6%
Backs	All backs	43.6–56.3%
	Half-back (scrum half)	7.3–11.8%
	Five-eight (fly-half)	4.5–14.7%
	Inside centre (2nd five) and outside centre	5.3–19.9%
	Left wing and right wing	4.7–14.6%
	Fullback	2.9–14.7%

* Data provided by seven studies[131]

other forwards. Together with the props, the hooker experiences the most force during the engagement of a scrum.[132] In 1983, a study of schoolboy rugby, again in South Africa, found that 40 per cent of injuries sustained by a hooker were to the neck, and twenty-five years later in Australian youth rugby it has been reported that front-row forwards are still at significantly greater risk of neck injury than other positions.[133]

8. What Other Factors Affect the Risk of Injury?

Foul play contributes very little to the incidence of injury at school level, with a range of between 1 and 8 per cent.[134] Foul play that causes injury includes high tackles, spear tackles, charging into another player, knocking a player down without trying to grasp their legs, or 'studding' someone while they are lying on the ground. These offences should all result in disciplinary action as they can cause serious injuries. But the vast majority of injuries in school level rugby arise from the structure of the game itself.

Studies have consistently shown a higher incidence of school level injuries with older age groups.[135] It is unlikely that age in itself is a risk factor for injury, but rather it is a reflection of the greater aggression, more competitive nature, faster pace and larger (and often unmatched) physiques involved in the contact elements of the sport. There is also a trend for young players to bulk up physically and hence players may be getting heavier.

The incidence of school rugby injury is always considerably greater in matches than in training. This is likely to be the result of the more competitive and aggressive nature of match play and the fact that a large amount of training is spent in non-contact activity.[136] The period of the school rugby season is strongly associated with injury rates. A greater number of injuries are consistently recorded at the start of the rugby season in comparison with mid-season and it is most likely that this is caused by insufficient pre-season training and a subsequent lack of player conditioning for the opening matches.[137]

9. What Steps Can Be Taken by Children and Schools to Prevent Injuries?

If a child is going to play rugby, the next question is what can be done to minimise the risk? Injury prevention needs to start before the playing season begins. Most injuries occur early on in the season, probably because children will have just returned to school from their summer break when it is likely that their levels of physical activity will have been substantially less than that which is enforced at school. As a result, fitness levels will be lower and bodies will be out of condition for the physical demands placed upon them in a high-paced contact sport. A graduated return to competitive play following the summer break is recommended to ensure a high-level of pre-match fitness, and schools have a duty of care and so a responsibility to ensure this. Some schools have already introduced pre-season training during the summer break. If a keen rugby player is at a school which does not offer pre-season training then parents should raise the matter as an inadequacy of the sport curriculum.

The focus of pre-season training sessions should be on safe play, with particular attention to techniques for safe scrummaging, safe tackling and safe falling. A questionnaire-based survey published in 1996 on 2,330 schoolboy rugby players from twenty-five schools in South Africa to establish how ready young players were for their first physical competitive game of the season found them to be very poorly prepared with insufficient knowledge of injury prevention.[138] It is down to rugby coaches to remedy this. They must be very well versed in injury prevention. Before the season starts they should provide players with evidence-based education, conditioning and training.

There are examples of existing initiatives along these lines. RugbySmart is an innovative compulsory educational programme, developed in 2001 in New Zealand, designed to equip community rugby coaches and referees with the best knowledge available on injury-prevention strategies.[139] This includes techniques to minimise injury risk during the contact phases of the game, pre-season physical conditioning and the appropriate management of injuries.[140] The compulsory workshops and training CDs educate coaches, who then use this knowledge to influence player attitudes, behaviour and technique.

RugbySmart has been found to significantly reduce moderate and serious injuries to the neck, spine, leg and knee. A higher percentage of players reported practising safe techniques in the contact phases of the game following the initiative.[141] Injury prevention programmes based on the educational principles of RugbySmart have now been developed in South Africa (BokSmart), Australia (SmartPlay) and Scotland (Are You Ready to Play Rugby?). However, unlike RugbySmart, none of these initiatives has yet been comprehensively evaluated, so it is not known if they have actually reduced injuries.

10. Will Protective Equipment like Mouth Guards and Head Guards Make a Child Safer?

Despite the development of protective kit, there is a lack of evidence to support its use.[142] The exception is the use of mouth guards (gum shields) that can prevent orofacial injuries to the mouth and teeth.[143] Mouth guards separate the upper and lower teeth and act as a shock absorber to large forces that could otherwise lead to serious dental injuries, such as fractured teeth. Unfortunately there is no compelling evidence that mouth guards protect against concussion.[144]

There are various types of mouth guard and the cost varies substantially. A randomised controlled trial of 301 players of Australian rules football comparing the protection offered against head and orofacial injuries from custom-fitted mouth guards with over-the-counter 'boil and bite' type or no mouth guard at all showed a significant reduction in risk for those who wore custom-fitted mouth guards.[145]

In New Zealand, the wearing of mouth guards became mandatory at all levels of rugby over a decade ago. An evaluation showed a 43 per cent reduction in claims for dental injuries to the New Zealand injury compensation system, the Accident Compensation Corporation (ACC), amounting to a potential saving of NZ$1.87 million.[146] Yet the wearing of fitted mouth guards is not compulsory for schoolchildren playing rugby in the UK.[147] The British Dental Association and the British Orthodontic Society have both lobbied for the mandatory use of mouth guards in school contact sport. It is important for parents to be aware that some dental insurance plans will not pay out if a mouth guard has not been worn during a match or training session.[148]

Some UK schools have made the wearing of mouth guards compulsory on their own initiative, but many others have not. In our study of rugby injuries in Scottish schools one in eight children did not wear mouth guards.[149] In a questionnaire sent to the parents of 1,111 children aged nine to thirteen from twenty-five schools in Ireland, of which approximately half responded, it was found that just one in five children were using mouth guards during sport and less than one in three schools and sports clubs had a policy on it.[150] Where schools did have a policy, significantly more children used mouth guards. We believe the wearing of mouth guards should be mandatory for rugby in all schools.

The effectiveness of head protection, such as scrumcaps, is much more controversial. Although there is evidence that headgear reduces superficial head injuries, it is generally accepted that there is no conclusive evidence that it offers any protection against concussion.[151]

Ironically, young players think that protective headgear allows them to play more aggressively and tackle harder, believing themselves unsusceptible to injury. This kind of attitude may be resulting in a greater number of injuries rather than reducing the impact of the high-intensity contact elements of the sport.[152]

11. Are Injuries a Big Reason for Children Giving Up Rugby?

Surveys show that a common reason for players giving up rugby is due to injury playing the game itself. A study of child and adult players in Scotland looked at the consequences of rugby injuries four years on from the 1993–94 season in which they occurred.[153] It found that 26 per cent of those surveyed had quit the sport because of rugby injuries, the most common reason. When broken down by age, 19 per cent of those younger than twenty gave up the sport because of a rugby injury, while interference in studies (23 per cent) and disillusionment with the game (20 per cent) accounted for slightly more. For the over-twenties, injury was the most frequently reported reason at 27 per cent,

Reasons why young players (<20yrs) give up playing rugby union

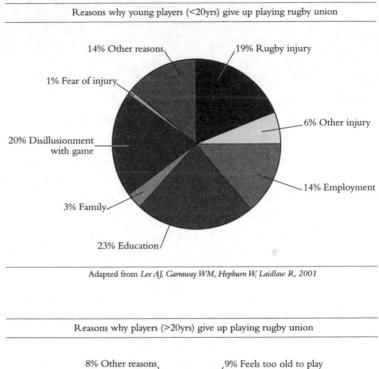

Adapted from *Lee AJ, Garraway WM, Hepburn W, Laidlaw R, 2001*

Reasons why players (>20yrs) give up playing rugby union

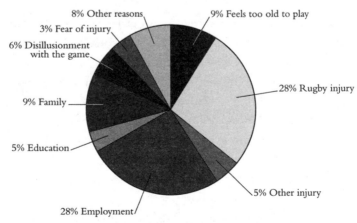

Adapted from *Lee AJ, Garraway WM, Hepburn W, Laidlaw R, 2001*

more than interference in employment (for instance, time off work) at 26 per cent (see pie charts).

12. What Are the Financial Costs of Rugby Injuries?

There are no reliable estimates in the UK of the average financial costs of child rugby injuries, including the cost to the NHS and to parents. However we can look at figures from New Zealand, where a tax-payer funded injury compensation system, the ACC, pays the costs of medical treatment, full rehabilitation and ancillary services such as transport and accommodation.[154] This system provides the impetus for reliable injury surveillance and data collection, something sorely lacking in the UK. In the 2005–6 financial year, a total of 4,384 claims for moderate or serious injuries sustained while playing rugby were made to the ACC. The costs totalled NZ$31,472,702. This amounts to NZ$7,179 per claim for a moderate or serious injury, or £2,871 (using the approximate currency exchange rate in 2005 of NZ$2.5 to £1). These figures include players of all ages and of course the costs of healthcare are not identical between the UK and New Zealand. However, the New Zealand example is enough to give a sense of the substantial financial costs of rugby injuries.

13. Can a Parent Withhold Consent for Their Child to Play, Especially in Schools Where Rugby Is Compulsory?

A school should not force a child to play competitive rugby. If a school insists that your child play against your

or your child's wishes, first make clear that you do not give
your consent. If this does not work there are strategies that
you can employ, such as asking for the data the school has
collected on past injury and risk, using the school's complaints procedure; also contact the school governors, the
parent–teacher forum, the schools inspector Ofsted and
the national Children's Commissioner. If your child is at
a private school it may be more difficult depending on the
contract you have signed.

There are a couple of relevant legal principles to be
aware of if your child is being forced to play. The first
is that children have rights under the United Nations
Convention on the Rights of the Child. This is an international treaty which the UK agreed to adhere to in 1991.
It means that all public bodies in the UK should respect,
protect and fulfil the rights of children. The UK's four
Children's Commissioners are there to help make sure this
happens. The UN Committee on the Rights of the Child,
which monitors countries' compliance with the treaty, has
said that as well as public bodies (like state schools), the
government must ensure that 'non-State service provid-
ers', like private schools and clubs, operate in accordance
with the Convention, 'thus creating indirect obligations on
such actors'. It has also said that the state 'continues to be
bound by its obligations under the treaty, even when the
provision of services is delegated to non-State actors'.[155]

The Convention does not mention sport expressly,
but the right to 'engage in play and recreational activities
appropriate to the age of the child' is recognised in Article
31.[156] Every child who is capable of forming his or her own
views has the right to express them freely in all matters and

they must be 'given due weight in accordance with the age and maturity of the child' (Article 12).[157] If a child expresses a desire to not play rugby, this should be given due weight.

The Convention says governments must 'take all appropriate legislative, administrative, social and educational measures to protect the child from all forms of physical or mental violence, injury or abuse, neglect or negligent treatment, maltreatment or exploitation, including sexual abuse, while in the care of parent(s), legal guardian(s) or any other person who has the care of the child' (Article 19).[158] UNICEF (the United Nations Children's Fund) says this means a child has 'the right to be protected from being hurt and mistreated, physically or mentally'.[159] Children also have the right to get information that is important to their health and well-being (Article 17).

The key in all of this – 'a primary consideration' (Article 3) – is what is in the best interests of the child. This applies to 'all actions concerning children, whether undertaken by public or private social welfare institutions, courts of law, administrative bodies or legislative bodies' (Article 3). Ultimately it is parents that have 'primary responsibility for the upbringing and development of the child' (Article 18).[160]

The second important legal concept that parents should be aware of is the 'duty of care' owed by those who are acting *in loco parentis* (in place of a parent). It is well established that schools, clubs and sporting associations have to take reasonable care of the children they are in charge of. This duty can apply, for example, at common law or by contract (such as where a private school contracts with parents). The UK Supreme Court has recently decided that this duty cannot be delegated, so schools have a positive duty to protect their children from harm and this applies to both school staff and to anybody the school makes a contract with to deliver sports for the children. This is exceptional, and one of the reasons the judge Lord Sumption gave for imposing this duty was because of the 'very substantial' control involved in the school-pupil relationship.[161]

Although educational establishments have a duty of care, whether they have sufficient understanding of the current data on rugby injuries to ensure parents and players give informed consent to play is highly doubtful. The invalidity of children consenting to the risk of injury from school rugby has already been documented in legal literature, particularly in schools where it is compulsory for children to play competitively.[162] If parents mention these legal principles they may find it easier to convince the school that their child should not be made to play rugby and should be given a safer alternative.

14. What Questions Should a Parent Put to a School About Its Injury Procedures?

If you are a parent with a child who plays rugby, asking the school specific questions about its injury procedures may not only help you to protect your child but also alert the school to possible shortcomings in the way it looks after all the children under its duty of care. A good question to ask is whether the school collects injury data and assesses the risk of rugby injuries, and whether it makes staff, pupils and parents aware of this information. The school should be able to give you the number of injuries in a season for each sport; the proportion of children and players injured each year; the type of injuries sustained and when they occurred during the game. The reality is that schools rarely collect this data, which raises the question of how they can allow high-impact collision games to proceed without even knowing how great the risk is.

Our own study of the epidemiology of school rugby injuries assessed the feasibility of a community-based rugby injury surveillance system for schools. The data we used was collected by a 'data champion', who took responsibility for co-ordinating all the relevant injury and exposure data for their particular school. Injury report forms were predominantly completed by non-medical staff, which is common practice for community-based epidemiological studies. The results and evaluation of our study confirmed that a community-based rugby injury surveillance system in schools is feasible and should be strongly advocated. Schools could set this up, if they wanted to.

In America there are laws covering concussion in sports in over forty states. These laws vary, with subtle differences between states, but tellingly many consistencies.[163] Although focused on concussion, they provide a useful basis for establishing what should be good practice for schools in dealing with all sports injuries. Informed by these laws, here are some examples of questions that concerned parents might wish to ask schools or rugby clubs:

Coach education:

- Do you require your rugby coaches to be educated regarding the most likely rugby injuries? What injuries are covered?

- Does that education involve specific training that must be renewed within stipulated time frames?
- Do you require formal training in a classroom or online? Or do you consider an information sheet sufficient?
- Who certifies the conduct, completion and renewal of training?

Parent and child education:

- Do you require children and parents to be educated about the most likely rugby injuries?
- If not, do you offer any level of education to them?
- If you require or offer any education, what does it consist of?
- Are parents required to sign anything, such as an information sheet?

Removal-from-play and return-to-play criteria:

- Some injuries require removal-from-play, such as concussion as specified under the Zurich consensus.[164] For what injuries, if any, does your school or club require removal from play?
- Who makes the evaluation?
- Do you require the suspicion of the relevant injury, signs or symptoms, loss of consciousness or something else?
- What criteria do you adopt for determining the return-to-play and who makes that evaluation?
- Do you have a sideline evaluation protocol?

Health care practitioner standards:

- Who evaluates, treats and clears children who have sustained injuries?
- Do you require them to be specifically trained to recognise and manage any particular injuries, such as concussion?

Baseline testing:

- Do you require pre-season cognitive baseline testing to establish a marker of a child's brain function before any potential concussion, which can then be used as a comparison should a brain injury occur?
- If so, what test do you use and who administers it?

Incentives and disincentives:

- Do you offer or impose any incentives or disincentives to minimise injuries? For example, can your coach or trainer have his or her licence suspended or revoked?

15. Where Can Parents Find Help?

There are a number of institutions and organisations which have overlapping responsibilities for the safety of schoolchildren and rugby injuries, as set out in Appendix 6. These may be able to help parents depending on the circumstances. There are also charities dedicated to helping those who have sustained rugby injuries, such as the Hearts and Balls Charitable Trust, the Murrayfield Centenary Fund in Scotland, the RFU's Injured Player Foundation

in England, the Welsh Rugby Charitable Trust and the
IRFU's Charitable Trust in Ireland.

16. What Can Be Done to Improve the Monitoring of Injuries in Rugby and Other Sports?

We identified nine sources of injury data across the UK that
have the potential to collect data on sporting injury and
rugby injuries in children and adolescents. These sources,
shown in Table 9, also reveal the fragmented nature of data
collection and the agencies with responsibilities.

Only two of the nine sources that collect and report
data complied with the World Health Organisation core
minimum dataset standards for injury surveillance. These
were HASS and LASS in England, which were discontinued by the Department of Trade and Industry discontinued
in 2002, and AWISS in Wales. Only these had collected any
information on sports injuries but this was limited to the
type of sport and exercise activity undertaken at the time of
injury. No further details regarding the sports injury were
recorded. Three of the data sources, HES, PEDW, and ISD,
were based on hospital admission records and therefore
only represented the most severe of injuries. The Health
and Safety Executive's *Reporting of Injuries, Diseases and
Dangerous Occurrences Regulations 1995* (RIDDOR) was
a potentially useful source of data on youth sport injuries
as it covered the whole of the UK population, including school pupils. However, Health and Safety Executive
school data and analyses were not routinely available even
though injuries in children and adolescents frequently
occur during school sports.

Table 9 Description of UK injury data sources covering children and adolescents (0–19 years)[165]

Dataset	Agency responsible for data collection	Source of funding	Data collection method	Population coverage / sample size
NHS Hospital Episode Statistics (HES)	Secondary Uses Service (SUS) [under the National Programme for IT]	UK Government	Routinely collected	Every NHS emergency department attendee and inpatient in England
Patient Episode Database for Wales (PEDW)	Health Solutions Wales	National Assembly for Wales	Routinely collected	Every NHS inpatient in Wales and Welsh patients in NHS hospitals in England
SMR datasets	Information Services Division NHS Scotland (ISD)	Scottish Government	Routinely collected	Every NHS inpatient in Scotland
Reporting of Injuries, Diseases and Dangerous Occurrences Regulations 1995 (RIDDOR)	Health and Safety Executive (HSE)	UK Government	Routinely collected	Working population of Great Britain plus off shore oil and gas industry including all school pupils / students
All Wales Injury Surveillance System (AWISS)	Health Solutions Wales	National Assembly of Wales	Surveillance system	All injured people attending A&E departments across most of Wales
Home and Leisure Accident Surveillance System (HASS and LASS) [discontinued in 2002]	Department of Trade and Industry, data now held by The Royal Society for the Prevention of Accidents (RoSPA)	UK Government via the former DTI (RoSPA funding for 5 years, 2003–08)	Surveillance system	All injured people attending sample of between 16 and 18 hospitals (excludes road traffic and work injuries)
Y-CHIRPP [discontinued in 2006]	A&E department, Royal Hospital for Sick Children, Yorkhill, Glasgow	NHS	Surveillance system	All children under 16 years presenting to Yorkhill A&E with an injury
Health survey for England	Department of Health (DH)	DH	Survey	There were 3,993 children aged 0–15 years interviewed in 2001 and 8067 interviewed in 2002
Scottish Health Survey	Scottish Executive Health Department (SEHD)	SEHD	Survey	There were 3,324 children under 16 years interviewed in 2003 (non-fatal injuries which do not result in long-term hospital admission)

Any UK-wide injury surveillance system based on emergency department attendance is going to miss many of the less serious injuries. Studies in the UK and Australia have demonstrated that up to 75 per cent of sports injuries are not treated at an emergency department or hospital.[166] In our study of rugby union injuries in Scottish schools, just under half of all injuries would have been unrecorded if A&E attendance was a stipulation for inclusion.[167] In fact the present situation is such that just one of the thirty-seven injuries we recorded would be reported to the ISD Scotland because only injuries that are serious enough to require hospital admission are noted.

It is the responsibility of government to ensure that schools fully record details of all injuries that happen to their pupils in school time, and that this information is properly reported to the Health and Safety Executive and agencies with responsibility for children. To capture the widest range of injuries with respect to severity, injury type, age group, and gender it is necessary to collect data at the point of injury.[168] This information should then be made available to a regional authority and go onto a UK-wide injury database, based on a national injury surveillance system, from which users could access the information to guide injury prevention.

Sports injuries systems have been established in schools in Canada and the US and are feasible.[169] Government action is required to implement data monitoring on all injuries including sports and rugby injuries in A&E departments, GP surgeries and schools. Parents, coaches and teachers must play a role in making this happen.

Part III
Peroration

More than thirty years ago the *British Medical Journal* ran a series of letters and editorials on the topic of the failure of sporting bodies and government departments to monitor rugby injuries. This debate was triggered by Frank d'Abreu, a sportsman, a surgeon and a distant relative of mine. He wrote:

Neglect of sports medicine:

Sir, your leading article on rugby injuries to the cervical cord (18 June 1977, p. 1556), will, I hope, be read and studied by all those interested in sports medicine. There is far less official notice taken of unacceptable injuries in rugby than in boxing and horse racing. In these two sports all serious injuries have to be reported to the governing bodies and it is comparatively easy to compile annual statistics proving the efficacy of preventive measures instituted as a result of a study of these figures.

I do not feel that the figures quoted in your article, in the absence of compulsory notification of serious injuries in rugby to a national authority, give a complete picture of the unacceptable injuries in amateur rugby football, though such figures are obtainable for professional rugby. It is evident also that your article contains no figures at all for English rugby, and I cannot but feel, as you do, that exact figures from Wales, Scotland, Ireland, and South Africa are hard to find and are by no means complete.

Your article highlights the necessity for the appointment of properly qualified medical advisers to the various governing bodies in sport at a national level, with the authority to recommend measures to cut down, if not eliminate, the incidence of unacceptable injuries and death. Great Britain is the only member country of the EEC which has no centre

for training in sports medicine in spite of the directive of the
Council of Ministers of the EEC on 26 October 1973 that all
countries in the European Community should establish these.
It is perhaps high time that the Minister for Sport takes action
in this matter to bring us in line with other nations.

Frank d'Abreu

The editorial article to which Frank referred is worth
reproducing here (BMJ, 18 June 1977):

Rugby injuries to the cervical cord:

June may seem an inappropriate month in which to consider rugby injuries. Yet a recent inquest has highlighted the
danger of new techniques in the game, and the summer may
be an appropriate time to consider whether any changes in the
rules are needed.

The game of rugby has evolved slowly as a hard contact
sport and some injuries are inevitable. Nevertheless, when
these are severe enough to cause permanent disability or
death we have a duty to examine both their incidence and
causes. We know that injuries to the cervical cord in rugby
footballers are rare, but exact figures of the incidence are
hard to find. In Ireland between 1959 and 1963 there were
estimated to be five serious injuries to the cervical spine, two
of them fatal, with 10,000 players turning out per season.
In Scotland between 1955 and 1965 only one fatal injury to
the cervical spine was recorded in a playing population of
11,000. The Welsh Rugby Union recorded two fractures
of the cervical spine, one resulting in complete permanent
paralysis and the other with partial residual paralysis, occurring between 1945 and 1964 in a population of 18,000 to
20,000 players.[1]

A recent article from South Africa[2] has described 20 patients who sustained cervical cord injuries while playing rugby. The patients came from an estimated total of 44,766 senior and schoolboy players and the injuries occurred over 12 years. Six players died, their ages ranging from 14 to 43. The injuries fell into two groups: those sustained while tackling (60%) and those while scrimmaging (40%). The nature of the tackling injuries varied, including fracture-dislocation of the cervical spine, compression fractures of vertebral bodies, fracture of the neural arch of C2, fracture of a spinous process, and two in which there was no radiological evidence of injury. The injuries in the scrimmaging group were more uniform: seven out of eight sustained a fracture-dislocation of the cervical spine with bilateral locking of the facet joints, while the other had locking on one side only. This injury is caused by a combination of flexion and rotation of the cervical spine and is likely to lead to paralysis and death. Typically it occurs when the scrum collapses, with the front row being the main victims.

Tackling and scrimmaging are integral parts of rugby, and any dramatic change in the laws (such as three- or five-man scrums) would drastically alter the game. Sound tackling techniques should be taught and ingrained at school with specific attention to the position of the head. Rigorous refereeing is needed when there is dangerous tackling, particularly with the high, stiff arm – a very dangerous foul – and offending players should be heavily penalised, even to the extent of sending them off. 'Lowering' in the front row of the scrimmage by either prop forward, more often the tight head, is often a forerunner to a collapsed scrum. Though this offence has been penalised more harshly recently, it should be recognised as serious enough to warrant dismissal of one or both offending players from the pitch. All referees must be briefed

in the tricks of modern scrimmaging and made fully aware of
the hazards of dangerous play. We can base any action only on
reliable information, and to access the real size of the problem
the circumstances of serious spinal injuries and death should,
perhaps, be reported to a central body by a designated club
official. Only then would the seriousness of certain offences
become obvious, and the need for stricter law enforcement or
changes in the laws become truly apparent.

The discussion that followed in the medical journals was
considerable, and all agreed something had to be done.[3]
What is so scandalous is that these calls from 1977 for
better injury monitoring and changes to the game still have
such resonance today.

We cannot fulfil the duty of care we owe children as
parents, doctors, teachers or coaches unless we know the
risks they are exposed to on the rugby field. If we take
children's rights seriously we must ensure that data is collected and studies are conducted to determine whether
the rewards of rugby outweigh the risks. Although sports
medicine is now an established speciality, there has been
little progress in this area since 1977, rather a wilful neglect.
And while sporting bodies are collecting data on professional players (possibly for insurance liability reasons),
they are not helping to systematically monitor injuries in
amateur or children's rugby.

It is extraordinary that injury, the major cause of morbidity and mortality among children and young people in the
UK, is not properly understood. Most injuries are avoidable if governments and responsible authorities would take
the trouble to care. Given that some of the toll of disability

falls on the health and social services, it is in the state's and the taxpayer's interest to protect children's health.

We do already have enough information to know that children's rugby, as it is currently played, is not acceptable. The way rugby is being coached and the rules under which it is played leave children vulnerable to serious injuries. There are alternatives short of a ban. The contact elements of the sport, especially the tackle and the scrum, are where most injuries occur, and a version of children's rugby that excludes these elements could be adopted. Children under eighteen years old could play the non-contact form of the game, tag rugby, for example. Rugby's defenders will make the argument that removing physical contact from the game would destroy its essence. But all games evolve and change over time. Preserving the essence of childhood is more important.

It is difficult to convince rugby's supporters of this. The game evokes strong passions and many prefer to deny the evidence. I have had several emails demanding that I end my 'campaign against rugby'. But my campaign is not against rugby itself; rather it is a public health professor's campaign to protect children from unnecessary harm.

In the end it is the parents and the children who carry the grief and burden of injury, not the teachers, the coaches, the referees or the rugby unions, who do not see these families in their darkest moments of hurt, misery, pain and terror.

Rugby is a sport dominated by business interests, well suited to a male-dominated, competition-obsessed society. It binds together powerful networks of the establishment; to challenge these bonds is to invite attack, marginalisation and alienation. But any parent would lay down their life for

their child. All we have to do is use the knowledge we have
to do what is right. If this book makes you change your
mind or want to ask more questions on behalf of your child
then it will have done its job.

Acknowledgements

Many people played a role in the writing of this book.

My initial motivation arose from a confluence of factors. My elder son, Hamish, was badly injured during a game of rugby. I felt a desire to protect his younger brother, Hector, a budding rugby star, from being exposed to the same risks. The weekly toll of injuries in Edinburgh schools over the autumn and spring terms has risen dramatically since I was at high school in Scotland in the 1970s, when I knew of only one such injury among local kids, a broken leg.

I owe a debt of gratitude to the many parents and boys I talked to at my son's school and to the other parents who have since phoned or met with me to share testimonies of their child's injuries. Sadly, sometimes these have resulted in long-term disabilities and, on two occasions, death. These parents have told me of their own personal struggles to come to terms with their child's suffering and their frustration at how little is being done. Every phone call or email I have received has made me realise how important it is to write this book and how lonely our battles to protect our children can be.

Some schools insist on rugby being compulsory, and parents are faced with a choice of allowing their child to be exposed to a risk of injury or removing them from school. And there is social pressure too. A neurophysician colleague asked me whether his son should play rugby at the French Lycée; he is an expert on head injury but confessed to intense pressure to conform. The mother of a brilliant young pianist at Haberdashers' Aske's School was told that rugby was no different from maths and English, an essential part of the curriculum. The parents of Benjamin Robinson, the fourteen-year-old who died from second-impact syndrome after being seriously concussed twice in quick succession, have mobilised a campaign of awareness around concussion and injury. They have achieved so much for all our children and have done a prodigious amount to wake up the rugby establishment.

During my research for this book I have encountered hostility and encouragement in less than equal measure. Among those who placed obstacles in my path are certain politicians and some rugby professionals, teachers, academics and doctors who behaved at times in ways that were despicable and extraordinary. I experienced at first hand bullying and intimidation and was frequently the target of ad hominem attack. There were those who resorted to personal abuse and smear and sought to undermine the science and rigour of our work. Over the course of ten years I have received hundreds of revolting, offensive, crude and sexist emails and tweets, usually contending that a woman who does not play rugby should not voice an opinion on the sport, let alone research it. But such irrational protest made the quest for data and knowledge more necessary.

At the other end of the spectrum, I have been contacted by thoughtful rugby players and coaches who have offered suggestions and advice or put forward counter-opinions in a polite and considered way. Their preparedness to engage in discussion and debate has been good and useful. There are even rugby heroes like Barry O'Driscoll and also Frank Heaven who have spoken out about injuries at some cost to themselves.

I owe special thanks to my friend Dr Ian Basnett, who broke his neck at the age of twenty-four playing rugby. He gave me insight into what it means to live with tetraplegia and how society further disables those with profound disabilities and the barriers and obstacles to normal living. He is an inspiration to me and to all who work with him in the field of public health.

I owe a deep debt of gratitude to my parents and large extended family in Scotland, England and Canada who never sought to dismiss my concerns and supported my sons and me when things got really hard, and when the press and a sporting establishment were at their most vicious. Above all my sons, Hamish and Hector, who have lovingly reconciled peer pressure, the love of the game and their mother's public health zeal.

Margo MacDonald MSP, herself once a brilliant athlete and P.E. teacher in her youth, and who developed disabling Parkinson's disease, championed our work through the Health and Sport Committee (as did Dr Ian McGee in Parliamentary questions). I pay tribute to her life-long commitment to transparency and truth. Wendy Sheehan gave me kind support at a crucial time when dealing with the school and various other authorities, as did Hedley Philpott, my sister Lorna, Kathy Harley and Richard Ibbetson, Dawn and Abdi Kermani, and Janet Murray. Simon Fraser for encouraging me initially. But special thanks go to David Price, James Lancaster, Sylvia Godden and to Neil Vickers for their unstinting encouragement always, to Sarah Richmond for suggesting the title, and to Chris Hill, rugby player par excellence, and his parents Jan and David. I especially value Tom Devine, Geoffrey Boulton, and Eric Scott, Jim and Margaret Cuthbert, Mick Power, Kath Melia and Jan Webb, whose many kindnesses and advice when I was dealing with the University of Edinburgh authorities I shall never forget.

Numerous colleagues have contributed in various ways to this book, often through research collaborations, and there are too many to mention. First and foremost among these I should thank Graham Kirkwood and Nikesh Parekh who have worked tirelessly on Part II and a range of other injury papers and briefings with me and who have been joined by Dianna Smith; Peter Roderick for the sections on law on the duty of care and the rights of the child; Prof. Stewart Hodges who authored the paper on risk and probability, and for assistance with referencing and other analysis, former Masters' students Andreas Freitag, Richard Oforio-Asenso and Sebastian Scharer. Part of the fun has been working with students who love the game, including medical students Francis Hanlon and Tom Chance.

Alex Nunns persuaded me that I had enough material to turn what was originally a compilation of studies on

Scottish struggles and in defence of academic freedom into a book focusing on rugby injuries. He stayed with it and helped me shape and edit the book; without him it would not have been finished. He is a brilliant and meticulous editor. Leo Hollis and Tariq Ali from Verso supported the idea as a necessary intervention and made it happen.

Every five or ten years, a bright young academic or doctor tries to pick up the cudgels on behalf of childhood injury but they are defeated by the entrenched attitudes and lack of funding for data collection, injury surveillance and prevention strategies. Clinicians and researchers like David Stone, Ronan Lyons, David Allen, Karim Brohi and others have made important contributions to the field of injury and trauma. But injury is a shamefully neglected area. Far too much research is focused on individual markers of risk and not enough is focused on the game and injury data collection and monitoring and primary prevention and rehabilitation. The UK Research Councils (funded by taxpayers) need to prioritise this Cinderella subject. The Centre for Trauma Sciences (C4TS) at Queen Mary and funded in part by Barts special trustees is a most necessary initiative and their funding of research fellows in public policy and prevention is vital to the whole field of injury and trauma.

Sadly, there is no money in preventing injury and trauma. The potential savings that could be made are not in cash, but in preventing pain and grief and disability. Because there is no money in public health research of this kind, academic freedom is vital. The rugby unions should not dictate the terms of research. Queen Mary University of London and the Centre for Trauma Sciences, under the leadership of Karim Brohi, provided the necessary academic environment to allow me to finish this book at a time when the whole medical and social care research enterprise is increasingly part of the medico-industrial complex driven by profit, commercialisation and performance measures.

The last word goes to David Allan, a brilliant and dedicated spinal surgeon at the Queen Elizabeth National Spinal Injuries Unit in the Southern General Hospital, Glasgow. He said to me that nothing will change until mothers demand it. It takes a special group of mothers to make a difference; I look forward to the day that change arrives.

Appendices

Appendix 1

Table 1 Translation of injury incidences to probabilities of injury (Parekh et al., 2012)[1]

Study	Injury definition	Population (schoolboys; ages – years)	Injury incidence	Average probability of injury to a player in a season
Nathan 1983 (South Africa)[2]	Injury prevents rugby participation for at least 1 week	<10–<19	8.4 per 1000 player-hours	14%
Sparks 1985 (UK)[3]	Injury prevents rugby participation for at least 1 week	<14	27.4 per 1000 player-hours	38%
		<15	54.2 per 1000 player-hours	61%
		<16	29.4 per 1000 player-hours	40%
		1st–4th XV	43 per 1000 player-hours	53%
Davidson 1987 (Australia)[4]	Injuries that required attention at the school sport's clinic	<13	13.6 per 1000 player-hours	21%
		14–15	18.4 per 1000 player-hours	28%
		>16	25.6 per 1000 player-hours	36%
Roux 1987 (South Africa)[5]	Injury prevents rugby participation for at least 1 week	<14–<19	7 per 1000 player-hours	12%
Durie 2000 (New Zealand)[6]	Injury causes player to leave field or complain at end of the match	<13	19.6 per 1000 player-hours	29%
		<14	20.8 per 1000 player-hours	31%
		<15	25 per 1000 player-hours	35%
		<16	25.9 per 1000 player-hours	36%
		<17	25 per 1000 player-hours	35%
		1st–5th XV	40.1 per 1000 player-hours	50%

Study	Definition	Age	Rate	%
Junge 2004 (New Zealand)[7]	Any physical complaint	14–18	129.8 per 1000 player-hours	90%
McIntosh 2005 (Australia)[8]	All match injuries	<13	41.4 per 1000 player-hours	52%
		<15	40.4 per 1000 player-hours	51%
		<18	52.6 per 1000 player-hours	60%
McIntosh 2010 (Australia)[9]	Injury required treatment or removal from pitch	<13	43.3 per 1000 player-hours	53%
		<15	56.3 per 1000 player-hours	63%
		<18	63 per 1000 player-hours	67%
Haseler 2010 (UK)[10]	Injury results in inability to take full part in future training or match play	<9	0 per 1000 player-hours	0%
		<10	6 per 1000 player-hours	9%
		<11	11 per 1000 player-hours	18%
		<12	23 per 1000 player-hours	33%
		<13	20 per 1000 player-hours	22%
		<16	28 per 1000 player-hours	39%
		<17	49 per 1000 player-hours	58%
Nicol 2010 (UK)[11]	Injury results in inability to take full part in future training or match play	11–18	10.8 per 1000 player-hours	17%

Appendix 2

Table 2 Summary of concussion studies. Concussion as a percentage of all injuries and incidence of concussion (figures are for rugby union and for matches only, unless otherwise stated)

Author / Year of publication	Country	Definition of injury	Definition of concussion	Concussion as a percentage of all injuries (n = number of concussions)	Incidence of concussion (95% confidence interval if given)
Baker et al. (2013) [1]	Ireland	Self-reported concussion	Self-reported concussion symptoms checked against Sports Concussion Assessment Tool version 2 (SCAT-2)	48% (n = 64) of players responding to survey had suffered at least 1 concussion	Not given
Collins et al. (2008) [2]	USA	Requiring medical attention by physician, trainer or emergency department; 1 or more days missed play	Not given	15.8% (n = 94) *	Not given
Durie and Munroe (2000) [3]	New Zealand	Unable to continue playing or reported injury at the end of a game: minor (able to play again in 7 days); moderate (unable to play for 1–3 weeks); severe (unable to play for more than 3 weeks)	Not given	3.2% (n = 6)	0.9 per 1,000 player-hours [1.5%] ∞
Fuller and Molloy (2011) [4]	International	Time-loss match injuries	Not given	4.7% (n = 9)	2.7 per 1,000 player-hours [4.6%] ∞
Gabbett (2008) [5] **	Australia	Player misses subsequent match	Not given	8.1% (n = 5)	4.6 (0.6, 8.6) per 1,000 player-hours [7.7%] ∞

Study	Country	Definition 1	Definition 2	Prevalence	Incidence
Haseler, Carmont and England (2010)[6]	England	Unable to return to play for at least 2 days	Concussion described to form completers as 'suffering from transient loss of consciousness, confusion, dizziness, nausea or visual disturbance following a head injury'	7.7% (n=3)	1.8 per 1,000 player-hours [3.1%]∞
Junge et al. (2004)[7]	New Zealand	Any physical complaint caused by rugby during training or match	Not given	2.9% (n=10) *	Not given
King (2006)**[8]	New Zealand	Any pain or disability suffered by a player during a match that required advice and / or treatment	Not given	6.8% (n=5)	14.7 (4.8, 34.2) per 1,000 player-hours [22.7%]∞
King et al. (2013)**[9]	New Zealand	Self-reported concussion	Concussion history items not defined, compared to post concussion symptom scale to establish baseline data	Under-15-year-olds (42 players): 4.1 (standard deviation 2.8) concussive incidents; 1.3 (0.5) loss of consciousness Under-17-year-olds (47 players): 3.8 (2.5) concussive incidents, 1.1 (0.3) loss of consciousness	Not given
Lee and Garraway (1996)[10]	Scotland	Sustained during training or match resulting in inability to play or train. Coded using ICD-9 classifications	Not given	12.2% (n=18)	10.6 (5.7, 15.4) concussions per 1,000 player-seasons [given as period prevalence]
Lewis and George (1996)[11]	England	Requiring attention on the pitch or after game or training session	Following a blow to the head, one or more of: loss of consciousness, loss of memory, confusion and disorientation; double/blurred/abnormal vision; giddiness or unsteadiness; vomiting; or headache	7.1% *	Not given

OR within 24 hours of blow to head one or more of: persistent headache; drowsiness leading to unconsciousness; irritability; confusion and loss of concentration; vomiting; or convulsions

Study	Country	Definition of injury	Definition of concussion	Concussion incidence	Rate
Marshall and Spencer (2001)[12]	USA	Injuries resulting in time lost from games or practice, all fractures and concussions recorded	Graded using Cantu Scale, loss of consciousness, disorientation, convulsions, dizziness, amnesia, disorientation or headache	24.6% (n=17) *	11.1 (4.8–17.4) per 1,000 player-games
McIntosh et al. (2010)[13]	Australia	Game injury – requiring on-field treatment or removal from game Missed game injury – player misses a game the following week, usually at least 7 days absence from competition	Defined by at least one of a list of 'concussion descriptors' on injury form including loss of consciousness, headaches, dizziness and post-traumatic amnesia	Game injuries: 10.8% (n=199) *** Missed game injuries: 7.8% (n=47) ***	Game injuries: 6.9 (4.4–9.4) per 1,000 player-hours [11.4%]∞ Missed game injuries: 1.6 (0.4–2.9) concussions per 1,000 player-hours [2.8%]∞
Nathan, Goedeke and Noakes (1983)[14]	South Africa	Severe enough to prevent player from play for at least 7 days	Not given	21.5% (n=17) *	Not given
Nicol et al. (2011)[15]	Scotland	Player unable to take a full part in future training or match play (taken from IRB definition)	Not given	16.2% (n=6) *	Not given
Roux et al. (1987)[16]	South Africa	Severe enough to prevent the player from returning to rugby for at least 7 days	All concussion injuries had to be reported regardless of ability to continue playing, concussion not defined	12.0% (n=59) *	Not given

		Concussion study			
Shuttleworth-Edwards et al. (2008)[17]	South Africa	Concussion study	Any alteration in neurological status occurring as a result of head-jarring trauma with or without loss of consciousness	n=135 concussions for the 1,147 players in the study	Not given
Sparks (1981)[18]	England	At least 1 week's absence from the game	Not given	5.2% (n=513) *	Not given
Sparks (1985)[19]	England	No definition given for injury, it was defined in prior study (see above Sparks 1981)	Loss of consciousness, however transient, caused by a blow to the head or neck	6.3% (n=49) *	Not given
Sugerman (1983)[20]	Australia (Australian Capital Territory, New South Wales and Queensland)	As reported by a player to the teacher, generally after a match	Not given	9.8% (n=46)	Not given
Upton, Roux and Noakes (1996)[21]	South Africa	No definition of injury or concussion given	No definition of injury or concussion given	888 (15.0% of all injuries reported) concussions reported by 471 players	Not given
Watson (1997)[22]	Ireland	Required medical treatment or disrupted training or matches	Not given	6.6% (n=8) *	Not given

* - matches and training combined

** - rugby league

*** - these percentages are of head, neck and face injuries only

∞ - Represents average probability of concussion to a player per season as calculated using the Parekh et al Poisson distribution model (27)

Appendix 3

Table 3 Details of studies included in this review

Author / Year of publication	Dataset details	Definition of injury	Definition of concussion / head injury	Who carried out the injury assessment	Age in years	Sex m= male; f=female	Time / Period	Country	Rules of game
Baker 2013[1]	Retrospective questionnaire survey on club and national academy elite youth rugby players, no time limit for recall	Concussion study only (not defined); participants' knowledge of concussion checked	Not defined	Self-reported by players	<20	m	2009–10 season	Ireland	Rugby union
Bird 1998[2]	Data collected from players prospectively throughout season via weekly phone calls	Medical attention required or player missed one game or practice session	Not defined	Player self-reported via weekly telephone interviews	<21	m	1993 season	New Zealand	Rugby union
Collins 2008[3]	Clubs completed weekly reports including injury details	Requiring medical attention by physician, trainer or emergency department and one or more days missed play	Not defined	Most were assessed by a doctor or other medical personnel such as an athletic trainer (93.0%)	13–19	m/f	2005–06 season	United States	Not given
Cusimano 2013[4]	Data extract from the Canadian Hospitals Injury Reporting and Prevention Program (CHIRPP) database (emergency department data)	Brain injury (minor closed head injury, concussion, intracranial injury)	Not defined	Hospital diagnosis	15–19	m/f	1990–09	Canada	Not given
Davidson 1978[5]	Data collected prospectively at a casualty station open during inter-school matches at a large Australian private school	Any injury however minor reported to casualty station	Not defined	Trained nurse	12–18	m	1969–76	Australia	Rugby union

Study	Data collection	Injury definition		Diagnosis	Age	Sex	Years	Country	Sport
Davidson 1987[6]	As above (follow-up study to Davidson 1978)	As above (follow-up study to Davidson 1978)	Not defined	Casualty room doctor and nurse	11–18	m	1969–86	Australia	Rugby union
Durie 2000[7]	Data collected at the injury clinic on the Monday following matches	Any injury sustained during a match, no restrictions, players instructed to attend injury clinic on Monday morning	Not defined	Doctor assessment at injury clinic	Not given	m	1998 season	New Zealand	Rugby union
Finch 1998[8]	Data extract from the Australian National Injury Surveillance Unit (emergency department data)	Any sport or active recreation injury case	Not defined	Hospital diagnosis	<15	Not given	1989–93	Australia	Rugby union, rugby league
Fuller 2011[9]	Data collected prospectively during four international competitions in 2008 and 2010	At least 2 days absence from games	Not defined	Team physician responsible for recording injury location and type	<20	m	2008 and 2010	International competitions	Rugby union
Gabbett 2006[10]	Data collected prospectively during training	Any pain or disability suffered by a player during training session which leads to player stopping training	Not defined	Head trainer	16–17	m	Not given	Australia	Rugby league
Gabbett 2008[11]	Match data collected prospectively	Player misses subsequent match	Not defined	Head trainer	17–19	m	2003–2006 seasons	Australia	Rugby league

Study	Data collection	Injury definition	Concussion definition	Injury recording	Age	Sex	Season	Country	Sport
Garraway 2000[12]	Club data collected prospectively and gathered weekly by visiting physiotherapists	Any injury sustained during training or match resulting in inability to play or train	Not defined	Not given	<19	m	1997–98 season	Scotland	Rugby union
Haseler 2010[13]	Data collected prospectively from one community rugby club	Any injury that prevents a player from taking a full part in all training and match play activities for at least one full day following day of injury	Concussion described to form-completers as suffering from transient loss of consciousness, confusion, dizziness, nausea or visual disturbance following a head injury	Injuries form completed by coaches or first aid staff. Formal diagnoses obtained for those players who attended GP or emergency department	<17	m	2008–09 season	England	Rugby union
Junge 2004[14]	Data collected prospectively via weekly player interview with doctor	Any physical complaint caused by rugby during training or match	Not defined	Doctor visited teams weekly to record injuries	14–18	m	March to August 2001	New Zealand	Rugby union
Lee 1996[15]	Data collected prospectively over season	Any injury sustained during training or match resulting in inability to play or train	Not defined	Injury recorded by teacher, school nurse or matrons. Additional information gained from parents and GP or hospital if appropriate	11–19	m	1993–94 season	Scotland	Rugby union

Study	Data collection	Injury	Definition	Diagnosis	Age	Sex	Dates	Country	Sport
Lewis 1996[16]	Data collected prospectively from games	Requiring attention on the pitch or after game or training session	Following a blow to the head, one or more of: loss of consciousness, loss of memory, confusion and disorientation; double, blurred or abnormal vision; giddiness or unsteadiness; vomiting; or headache. Or within 24 hours of blow to head one or more of: persistent headache; drowsiness leading to unconsciousness; irritability; confusion and loss of concentration: vomiting; or convulsions	Questionnaire completed by club doctor or physiotherapist	16–18	m/f	September 1992–April 1994 (two seasons)	England	Rugby union
MacLean 2012[17]	Data extracts from UK spinal injury units	Spinal cord injury	Not defined	Hospital diagnosis	14–18	m	1996–10	Great Britain and Ireland	Rugby union

Study	Data collection method	Injury definition	Concussion definition/grading	Concussion data collection	Age	Sex	Year	Country	Sport
Marshall 2001[18]	Data collected prospectively onto a custom made database	Injuries resulting in time lost from games or practice; all fractures and concussions recorded	Graded using Cantu Scale, loss of consciousness, disorientation, convulsion, dizziness, amnesia, disorientation or headache	Not given, concussions are monitored and reviewed by team physician	Not given	Not given	1998–2000 (three seasons)	USA	Rugby union
McIntosh 2010[19]	Data collected prospectively from matches	Game injuries: requiring on-field treatment or removal from game. Missed game injuries: player misses a game the following week	'Concussion descriptors' on injury form such as loss of consciousness, headaches, dizziness and post-traumatic amnesia	Injury data collected at games by university students, typically studying medicine, physiotherapy or sports science supplements with information from players doctor or team physiotherapist	<20	m	2002–03 (two seasons)	Australia	Rugby union
McManus 2004[20]	Data collected prospectively from training and games	Any injury sustained during training or match including being able to return to game	Not defined	Lead author attended all assessments and filled out RUIRFs	<16	m	26 weeks up to and including the 1997 National Championships	Australia	Rugby union
Nathan 1983[21]	Injury data collected weekly via missed game reports	Severe enough to prevent player from play for at least 7 days	Not defined	Self-reported player questionnaire, interviewed by study personnel	<19	m	1982 season	South Africa	Rugby union

					Age	Sex	Season	Country	Sport
Nicol 2011[22]	Data collected prospectively by school 'data champion'	Injury occurring during match or training resulting in player being unable to take a full part in future rugby training or match play	Not defined	Injury recorded/assessed by school-based data collector (majority were non-medical)	11–18	m/f	Second half of 2008–09 season	Scotland	Rugby union
Palmer-Green 2013[23]	Data collected prospectively from matches	Any injury that prevents a player from taking a full part in all training and match play activities for at least one full day following day of injury	Not defined	Schools: first team coach recorded match exposure and nurse/physician recorded injury data. Academy: match exposure recorded by strength and conditioning coach and injury data by physical therapist	16–18	m	2006–08 (two seasons)	England	Rugby union
Pringle 1998[24]	Data collected prospectively from matches with telephone follow-up over a 4-week period	Injury which impaired a player's performance	Not defined	Collection by trained observers (physiotherapy or science students with suitable training in anatomy and sports medicine); reports to experienced physiotherapy and lead author	6–15	m	Not given	New Zealand	Rugby league, rugby union

Study	Data collection	Definition of injury	Definition of concussion	Recorded by	Age	Sex	Year/season	Country	Sport
Roux 1987[25]	Data collected weekly following matches	Severe enough to prevent player from play for at least 7 days; all concussions recorded	Not defined	Teacher/coach completed one weekly form for all injuries, injured players completed individual injury report forms	<18	m	1983 (one 18-week season)	South Africa	Rugby union
Shuttleworth-Edwards 2008[26]	Data collected prospectively from matches	Concussive incident requiring follow-up	Any alteration in neurological status occurring as a result of head-jarring trauma with or without loss of consciousness	Doctor (four schools), nurse (one school)	Not given	m	2002–06	South Africa	Rugby union
Sparks 1981[27]	Data collected routinely by school doctor	At least one week's absence from the game	Not defined	Not given, paper written by school doctor	13–18	m	1950–79	England	Rugby union
Sparks 1985[28]	As above (follow-up study to Sparks 1981)	Not defined; defined in prior study (see above Sparks 1981[29])	Loss of consciousness, however transient, caused by a blow to the head or neck	Not given, paper written by school doctor	Not given	m	1980–83 (four seasons)	England	Rugby union
Sugerman 1983[30]	Data collected from matches and centralized monthly	As reported by player to the teacher, generally after match	Not defined	Teacher	Not given	m	1981 school season (April–July)	Australia	Rugby union
Upton 1996[31]	Data collected retrospectively via questionnaire survey	Not defined	Not defined	Self-completed player questionnaires	Not given	m	1991	South Africa	Rugby union

Study	Data collection	Injury definition		Personnel	Age	Period	Country	Sport
Usman 2013[32]	Data collected weekly via injury report forms	Injury such that player misses subsequent game	Not defined	Trainer, physiotherapists, physiotherapy student or sports science student	Not given	m	2004–08 (5 seasons)	Australia	Rugby union
Weir 1996[33]	Data collected retrospectively via questionnaire survey	Any pain, discomfort or incapacity during the preceding 12 months attributable to sport requiring at least two days absence from match or training	Not defined	Questionnaires completed under supervision of lead author	12–15	m/f	Not given	Ireland	Not given

Appendix 4

Table 4 Studies showing incidence of injury during training only, including number of players, number of injuries and exposure

Author and year of publication	Number of players	Number of injuries	Total exposure	Incidence of injury for training only
Gabbett 2006[1]	36	Not given	Not given	56.2 (35.7, 76.6) injuries per 1,000 player-hours
Junge 2004[2]	123	115	5,141 player-hours*	22.4 injuries per 1,000 player-hours
Nathan 1983[3]	Not given	29	25,110 player-hours	1.2 injuries per 1,000 player-hours
Roux 1987[4]	Not given	142	258,182 player-hours	0.55 injuries per 1,000 player-hours
Sparks 1985[5]	Not given	212	17,090 player-hours	12.4 injuries per 1,000 player-hours*
Bird 1998[6]	141	Not given	Not given	2.1 injuries per 100 player-practices
Collins 2008[7]	Not given	103	81,627 practice-exposures	1.3 injuries per 1,000 practice-exposures
Marshall 2001[8]	Not given	5	3,333 player-practices*	1.5 (0.2, 2.8) concussions per 1,000 player-practices

* Calculated post-hoc from figures in paper

Appendix 5

Table 5 List of organisations with overlapping responsibilities for the safety of schoolchildren and rugby injuries

United Kingdom
Health and Safety Executive
Redgrave Court,
Merton Road,
Bootle, Merseyside,
L20 7HS
Tel: 0845 300 9923
www.hse.gov.uk

Royal Society for the Prevention of Accidents
RoSPA House,
28 Calthorpe Road,
Edgbaston,
Birmingham,
B15 1RP
(Specific Scottish, Welsh and Northern Irish offices also listed on website)
Tel: 0121 248 2000
Email: help@rospa.com
www.rospa.com

England
Care Quality Commission
National Customer Service Centre,
Citygate,
Gallowgate,
Newcastle upon Tyne,
NE1 4PA
Tel: 0300 061 6161
Email: enquiries@cqc.org.uk
www.cqc.org.uk

Child Protection in Sport Unit
NSPCC National Training Centre,
3 Gilmour Close,
Beaumont Leys,
Leicester,
LE4 1EZ
(Welsh and Northern Irish offices also listed on website)
Tel: England and Wales: 0116 234 7278
Tel: Northern Ireland: 0203 222 4246
www.thecpsu.org.uk

Children's Commissioner
33 Greycoat Street,
London,
SW1P 2QF
Tel: 0207 783 8330
Email: info.request@childrenscommissioner.gsi.gov.uk
www.childrenscommissioner.gov.uk

Ofsted
Piccadilly Gate,
Store Street,
Manchester,
M1 2WD
Tel: 0300 123 1231
Email: enquiries@ofsted.gov.uk
www.ofsted.gov.uk

Rugby Football Union
Rugby House,
Twickenham Stadium,
200 Whitton Road,
Twickenham, Middlesex,
TW2 7BA
Tel: 0871 222 2120
www.rfu.com

Sport England
Victoria House,
Bloomsbury Square,
London,
WC1B 4SE
Tel: 0845 850 8508
Email: info@sportengland.org
www.sportengland.org

Scotland

Education Scotland
Denholm House,
Almondvale Business Park,
Almondvale Way,
Livingston,
EH54 6GA
Tel: 0141 282 5000
Email: enquiries@educationscotland.gov.uk
www.educationscotland.gov.uk

Safeguarding in Sport
Children 1st,
Sussex House,
61 Sussex Street,
Kinning Park,
Glasgow,
G41 1DY
Tel: 0141 418 5674
Email: safeguardinginsport@children1st.org.uk
www.children1st.org.uk

Scotland's Commissioner for Children and Young People
85 Holyrood Road,
Edinburgh,
EH8 8AU
Tel: 0131 558 3733
Email: inbox@sccyp.org.uk
www.sccyp.org.uk

Scottish Rugby
Murrayfield,
Edinburgh,
EH12 5PJ
Tel: 0131 346 5000
Email: feedback@sru.org.uk
www.scottishrugby.org

Sport Scotland
Doges,
Templeton on the Green,
62 Templeton Street,
Glasgow,
G40 1DA
Tel: 0141 534 6500
Email: sportscotland.enquiries@sportscotland.org.uk
www.sportscotland.org.uk

Wales

Children's Commissioner for Wales
Oystermouth House, Phoenix Way,
Llansamlet,
Swansea,
SA7 9FS
Tel: 0179 276 5600
Email: post@childcomwales.org.uk
www.childcom.org.uk

Estyn
Anchor Court,
Keen Road,
Cardiff,
CF24 5JW,
Tel: 0292 044 6446
Email: enquiries@estyn.gov.uk
www.estyn.gov.uk

Inspection Services Branch
Department of Education,
Room F29,
Rathgael House,
43 Balloo Road,
Rathgill, Bangor,
BT19 7PR
Tel: 0289 127 9726
Email: inspectionservices@deni.gov.uk
www.etini.gov.uk

Sport Wales
Sophia Gardens,
Cardiff,
CF11 9SW
Tel: 0845 045 0904
Email: info@sportwales.org.uk
www.sportwales.org.uk

Welsh Rugby Union
Millennium Stadium,
Westgate Street,
Cardiff,
CF10 1NS
Tel: 0844 249 1999
Email: info@wru.co.uk
www.wru.co.uk

Northern Ireland

Northern Ireland Commissioner for Children and Young People
Equality House,
7–9 Shaftesbury Square,
Belfast,
Country Antrim,
BT2 7DP
Tel: 0289 031 1616
Email: info@niccy.org
www.niccy.org

Sport Northern Ireland
House Of Sport,
Upper Malone Road,
Belfast,
County Antrim,
BT9 5LA
Tel: 0289 038 1222
Email: info@sportni.net
www.sportni.net

Ireland

Irish Rugby Football Union
10/12 Lansdowne Road,
Dublin 4,
Ireland
Tel: +353 (0) 1 647 3800
Email: info@irishrugby.ie
www.irishrugby.ie

Notes

Introduction

1. L. Abernethy, D. MacAuley, 'Impact of school sports injury', *British Journal of Sports Medicine*, 2003, 37(4) pp. 354–5.
2. Ibid. *See also* A. S. Goldberg, L. Moroz, A. Smith, T. Ganley, 'Injury surveillance in young athletes: a clinician's guide to sports injury literature', *Sports Medicine*, 2007, 37(3) pp. 265–78.
3. M. J. Shelly, J. S. Butler, M. Timlin, M. G. Walsh, A. R. Poynton, J. M. O'Byrne, 'Spinal injuries in Irish rugby: a ten-year review', *Journal of Bone and Joint Surgery*, 2006, 88(6) pp. 771–5. *See also* R. M. Durie, A. D. Munroe, 'A prospective survey of injuries in a New Zealand schoolboy rugby population', *New Zealand Journal of Sports Medicine*, 2000, 28(4) pp. 84–91.
4. Shelly et al., 'Spinal injuries in Irish rugby'.
5. A. Nicol, A. M. Pollock, G. Kirkwood, N. Parekh, J. Robson, 'Rugby union injuries in Scottish schools', *Journal of Public Health*, Oxford 2011, 33(2) pp. 256–61
6. A. Bull, 'Death of a schoolboy: why concussion is rugby union's dirty secret', *Guardian*, 13 December 2013.
7. 'Ben Robinson's rugby death is first of its kind in Northern Ireland', bbc.co.uk, 25 September 2013.
8. 'Death of a schoolboy', *Guardian*, 13 December 2013.

9. 'Promising young student sues for €5m after suffering brain damage while playing school rugby match', *Irish Independent*, 4 March 2014.

10. http://www.rfu.com/news/2005/november/news-articles/rugbyfootballunionannouncesrecordfinancialresults

11. RFU Annual Report 2013. *Available at*: http://www.rfu.com

12. Welsh Rugby Union. The Welsh Rugby Union Limited Annual Report 2005 and The Welsh Rugby Union Limited Annual Report 2013. *Available at*: http://www.wru.co.uk/

13. IRFU. Accounts & Statistics 2004/2005 and Annual Report 2012/2013. *Available at*: http://www.irishrugby.ie/

14. http://www.lagardere.com/fichiers/fckeditor/File/Relations_investisseurs/presentations_analystes/2011/PR_Lagardere_LU_250111.pdf

15. M. Phillip, 'Rugby-Six Nations attracts record TV viewing figures', Reuters.com, 22 March 2011.

16. Nicol et al., 'Rugby union injuries in Scottish schools'. *See also* K. M. Kaplan, A. Goodwillie, E. J. Strauss, J. E. Rosen, 'Rugby injuries: a review of concepts and current literature', *Bulletin of the New York University Hospital for Joint Diseases*, February 2008, 66(2) pp. 86–93.

17. International Rugby Board, '119 countries ... 6.6 million players', irb.com. *Available at*: http://www.irb.com/mm/Document/AboutIRB/IRBOrganisation/02/07/03/26/irb-dev-glob-map.pdf.

18. FIFA, 'Big Count', fifa.com. *Available at*: http://www.fifa.com/worldfootball/bigcount/index.html.

19. R. Kitson, 'English rugby union's lost decade', *Guardian*, 1 November 2013.

20. 'Active People Survey 7', Sportengland.org, 13 June 2013.

21. 'Unintentional Injuries', Information Services Division Scotland, 25 February 2014. *Available at*: http://www.isdscotland.org/Health-Topics/Emergency-Care/Publications/2014-02-25/2014-02-25-UI-Report.pdf.

22. 'Women's rugby has gone from strength to strength over recent

years and participation is currently at an all-time high with nearly 14,000 women and girls currently registered as playing each week', from the Rugby Football Union website, 'Women's Rugby', rfu.com.

23. H. Briggs, 'Rise in child obesity-related hospital admissions', BBC.co.uk, 13 June 2013.

24. 'Briefing note: obesity and life expectancy', National Obesity Observatory, August 2010, noo.org.uk. *See also* 'How much does obesity cost the NHS?' Fullfact.org, 26 May 2011.

25. I. Male, 'Safeguarding children in sport: a paediatricians's perspective', Celia Brackenridge, Tess Kay, Daniel Rhind, eds, *Sport: Children's Rights and Violence Prevention: A Sourcebook on Global Issues and Local Programmes*, London: Brunel University Press, 2012, pp. 40–8.

26. 'Unintentional child injuries in the WHO European region', World Health Organisation, 2006, who.int. *See also* D. H. Stone, 'The continuing global challenge of injury', *British Medical Journal*, 20 June 2001 (322) pp. 1557–8. *See also* G. Kirkwood, A. M. Pollock, 'Preventing injury in childhood', *British Medical Journal*, 19 June 2008 (336) pp. 1388–9.

27. 'BMA Renews Calls for Boxing Ban', BBC.co.uk, 3 May 1998.

28. 'Boxing Risk to Children', BBC.co.uk, 28 January 1999.

29. Ibid.

30. T. Bowling, 'Facing uncertainty: local governments and the precautionary principle', National Sea Grant Law Center, 2013, olemiss.edu.

31. On tax breaks, *see* HM Treasury and HM Revenue and Customs, 'Newly expanded grassroots sports relief to help local sports clubs', GOV.uk, 23 November 2013.

32. W. M. Garraway, A. J. Lee, S. J. Hutton, E. B. Russell, D. A. Macleod, 'Impact of professionalism on injuries in rugby union', *British Journal of Sports Medicine*, 2000, 34(5) pp. 348–51. *See also* S. J. Jones, R. A. Lyons, J. Sibert, R. Evans, S. R. Palmer, 'Changes in sports injuries to children between 1983 and 1998: comparison of case series', *Journal of Public Health*, 2001, 23(4) pp. 268–71. *See*

also J. G. MacLean, J. D. Hutchison, 'Serious neck injuries in U19 rugby union players: an audit of admissions to spinal injury units in Great Britain and Ireland', *British Journal of Sports Medicine*, 2012, 46(8) pp. 591–4.

33. 'Being Safe and Protected from Harm', Equality and Human Rights Commission, 2013, equalityhumanrights.com.

34. P. David, *Human Rights in Youth Sport: A Critical Review of Children's Rights in Competitive Sports*, Routledge, 2005.

35. 'Convention on the Rights of the Child', United Nations Human Rights: Office of the High Commissioner for Human Rights, 2 September 1990 in accordance with Article 49, ohchr.org.

36. Ibid.

37. Ibid.

38. 'The Evolving Capacities of the Child', Child Rights International Network, 2005, crin.org.

39. UNICEF, 'The Convention on the Rights of the Child, 2013', unicef.org. *Available at*: http://www.unicef.org/crc/files/Protection_list.pdf.

40. Ibid.

41. K. Belson, 'N.F.L agrees to settle concussion suit for $765 million', *New York Times*, 29 August 2013.

42. S. Smith, 'Duerson brain tissue analysed: suicide linked to brain disease', cnn.com, 3 May 2011.

43. J. Kass, 'American football industry is on its deathbed', *Chicago Tribune*, 24 April 2013. S. Wagg, B. Wheaton, C. Brick, J. Caudwell, *Key Concepts in Sports Studies*, Sage, 2009.

44. 'Derek Boogaard's family files lawsuit against NHL', cbc.ca, 12 May 2013.

45. J. Kass, 'American football industry'.

46. F. Coalter, *A Wider Social Role for Sports*, Routledge, 2007.

47. 'Ken Clarke's BAT role makes him unfit for leadership', Action on Smoking and Health (ASH), 31 August 2005, news release at ash.org.uk.

48. 'Key dates in the history of anti-tobacco campaigning', Action on Smoking and Health (ASH), ash.org.uk.

49. R. Roxby, 'Smoking ban's impact'. *See also* M. Sims, R. Maxwell, A. Gillmore, 'Short-term impact of smokefree legislation in England on emergency hospital admissions for asthma among adults: a population-based study', *Thorax*, July 2013, 68(7) pp. 619–24. *See also* N. McDermott, 'Cigarette sales fell by seven per cent following smoking ban', *Daily Mail*, 17 Septempber 2007. *See also* 'Smoking ban "cost pub takings"', bbc.co.uk, 17 December 2007. *See also* Christine Callum, Seán Boyle and Amanda Sandford, 'Estimating the Cost of Smoking to the NHS in England and the Impact of Declining Prevalence', *Health Economics, Policy and Law*, August 2010, 6(4) pp. 489–508.

50. 'Scotch Whisky industry challenges minimum pricing of alcohol', Scotch Whisky Association, 19 July 2012, scotch-whisky.org.uk.

51. 'Industry documents deveal the truth about alcohol advertising', Institute of Alcohol Studies (IAS), 2010. Available at: http://www.ias.org.uk/What-we-do/Publication-archive/Alcohol-Alert/Issue-1-2010/Industry-documents-reveal-the-truth-about-alcohol-advertising.aspx. *See also* G. Hastings, O. Brooks, M. Stead, K. Angus, T. Anker, T. Farrell, 'Failure of self regulation of UK alcohol advertising', *British Medical Journal*, 21 January 2010, (340) p. b5650.

52. 'BBC Panorama Alcohol Report Questions Industry Influence', alcoholpolicy.net, 3 August 2011.

53. S. Adams, 'Alcohol advisory body "stacked with drinks industry lobbyists"', telegraph.co.uk, 1 August 2011.

54. R. Doll, 'Mortality from lung cancer in asbestos workers', *British Journal of Industrial Medicine*, 1955, 12(2) pp. 81–6. *See also* 'Asbestos Ban History in the UK', Asbestos Victim Advice, 24 November 2010, asbestosvictimadvice.com. *See also* 'Government Asbestos Compensation Scheme Announced', Nelsons Solicitors, 21 September 2012, nelsonslaw.co.uk.

1. Another Injury, but Not Another Statistic

1. 'Are you ready to Play?' scottishrugby.org, 2013.
2. A. E. MacQueen, W. W. Dexter, 'Injury trends and prevention in rugby union football', *Current Sports Medicine Reports*, 2010, 9(3) pp. 139–43.
3. 'Working together to make Europe a safer place', European Association for Injury Prevention and Safety Promotion (EuroSafe), 2013. *Available at*: eurosafe.eu.com.
4. Vital events reference table published online by the General Register Office for Scotland, 2012. Available at: http://www.gro-scotland.gov.uk/statistics/theme/vital-events/general/ref-tables/index.html.
5. 'Unintentional Injuries', published by the Information Services Division (ISD), 2013, isdscotland.org. Available at: http://www.isdscotland.org/Health-Topics/Emergency-Care/Publications/.
6. 'Home safety', scotland.gov.uk. *Available at*: http://www.scotland.gov.uk/Topics/Justice/public-safety/17141/homesafety.
7. 'Child Safety Strategy: Preventing Unintentional Injuries to Children and Young People in Scotland', produced in support of the Child Safety Action Plan for Europe, by the Royal Society for the Prevention of Accidents (RoSPA) and the Child Accident Prevention Trust (CAPT), May 2007.
8. Scottish Health Survey, Scottish Government results, 2005.
9. G. Kirkwood, N. Parekh, A. M. Pollock, 'Preventing injury in children and adolescents', *Trauma*, 2010, 12(4) pp. 221–38.
10. J. H. Brooks, C. W. Fuller, 'The influence of methodological issues on the results and conclusions from epidemiological studies of sports injuries: illustrative examples', *Sports Medicine*, 2006, 36(6) pp. 459–72. *See also* Tom Geoghegan, 'Could rugby union take off in the US?', bbc.co.uk, 7 September 2011.
11 Nicol et al., 'Rugby union injuries in Scottish schools'. *See also* J. R. Silver, 'The impact of the 21st century on rugby injuries', *Spinal Cord*, 2002, 40(11) pp. 552–9.

12. Lyle J. Micheli, 'Enhancing safety in youth rugby', USA Rugby, 2003, jrbluesrugby.com.

13. R. R. Pate, M. G. Davis, T. N. Robinson, E. J. Stone, T. L. McKenzie, J. C. Young et al., 'Promoting physical activity in children and youth: a leadership role for schools: a scientific statement from the American Heart Association Council on Nutrition, Physical Activity, and Metabolism (Physical Activity Committee) in collaboration with the councils on Cardiovascular Disease in the Young and Cardiovascular Nursing', *Circulation*, 2006, 114(11) pp. 1214–24.

14. J. P. Nicholl, P. Coleman, B. T. Williams, 'The epidemiology of sports and exercise related injury in the United Kingdom', *The British Journal of Sports Medicine*, 1995, 29(4) pp. 232–8.

15. Nicol et al., 'Rugby union injuries in Scottish schools'.

16. Garraway et al., 'Impact of professionalism'.

17. P. Haylen, 'Spinal injuries in rugby union 1970–2003: Lessons and responsibilities', *Medical Journal of Australia*, 2004, 181(1) pp. 48–50.

2. Rugby's Web of Interests

1. A. M. Pollock, 'We have to tackle child injury on the sports field', *Herald*, April 2008.

2. 'History of the Border League', Border League. *Available at*: kingsofthesevens.net.

3. Scotland: International Rugby Board, 2013, irb.com. *Available at*: http://www.irb.com/unions/union=11000004/index.html.

4. 'Edinburgh University RFC', rugbyfootballhistory.com, 2007.

5. T. Collins, *Rugby's Great Split: Class Culture and the Origins of Rugby League Football*, Frank Cass Publishers, 1998, p. 6.

6. A. W. Howard, 'Injury in childhood: a vexingly simple problem', *Canadian Medical Association Journal*, 2006, 175(8) pp. 899.

7. 'BMJ bans "accidents" ', editorial, *British Medical Journal*, 2 June 2001, 332(2) p. 1320–1.

8. Kirkwood et al., 'Preventing injury in children'.

3. A Pilot Study of Injuries

1. A. Kervin, 'Tackling rugby safety issues head-on', telegraph.co.uk, 12 September 2011.
2. 'Male Under-16 Players in Under-18 Rugby', scottishrugby.org, May 2009.
3. Nicol et al., 'Rugby union injuries in Scottish schools'.
4. Ibid.
5. Garraway et al., 'Impact of professionalism'.
6. B. Gallagher, 'Six nations banking on RBS after extending sponsorship', *Daily Telegraph*, 24 January 2009. See also Harry Wilson, 'RBS has lost all the £46bn pumped in by the tax payer', *Daily Telegraph*, 27 February 2014.
7. 'The Way Forward: 2016 and Beyond Policy Initiatives', Scottish Rugby Union, December 2013, scottishrugby.org.

4. Marginalizing the Cause of Public Health

1. N. Parekh, S. D. Hodges, A. M. Pollock, G. Kirkwood, 'Communicating the risk of injury in schoolboy rugby: using Poisson probability as an alternative presentation of the epidemiology', *British Journal of Sports Medicine*, 2012, 46(8) pp. 611–3.
2. 'Call to ban rugby scrums in schools', bbc.co.uk, 4 July 2010. *See also* A. Mourant, 'Rugby and research: a happy collision', *Guardian*, 1 November 2010.
3. K. Khan, 'Crying wolf: When media reports distort research evidence', British Medical Journal Group Blogs, 7 September 2010. Available at: bmj.com.
4. Brooks, et al., 'A prospective study of injuries and training amongst the England 2003 Rugby World Cup squad' *British Journal of Sports Medicine* 39,5 (2005). *See also* CRISP season reports, available at: http://www.bath.ac.uk/health/projects/rfu-rugby-injury/reports-papers/.
5. Garraway et al., 'Impact of professionalism'.
6. J. Bourke, 'Rugby union should ban contested scrums', *British Medical Journal*, 2006, 332(7552) p. 1281. *See also* Jonathan

Wynne-Jones, 'Ban the scrum, says top rugby coach', independent. co.uk, 12 February 2006.

7. D. J. Carmody, T. K. Taylor, D. A. Parker, M. R. Coolican, R. G. Cumming, 'Spinal cord injuries in Australian footballers 1997–2002', *Medical Journal of Australia*, 2005, 182(11) pp. 561–4.

8. H. C. Burry, C. J. Calcinai, 'The need to make rugby safer', *British Medical Journal* (Clinical Research Edition), 1988, 296(6616) pp. 149–50.

9. J. Bourke, 'Rugby union should ban contested scrums'.

10. Garraway et al., 'Impact of professionalism'.

11. 'Experts clash on scrum safety', heraldscotland.com, 8 July 2010.

12. Centre for Sport and Exercise, Sports Medicine Centre at the University of Edinburgh, overview published online 31 March 2013. *Available at*: http://www.ed.ac.uk/schools-departments/ sport-exercise/fasic.

13. M. G. Dunnigan, A. M. Pollock, 'Downsizing of acute inpatient beds associated with private finance initiative: Scotland's case study', *British Medical Journal*, 2003, 326(7395) p. 905.

14. Consultant Profile on the SPIRE Edinburgh Hospitals website, 2013. Available at: http://www.spirehealthcare.com/edinburgh/ our-facilities-treatments-and-consultants/our-consultants/ mr-graham-m-lawson/.

15. SPIRE Edinburgh Hospitals homepage, 2013. Available at: http://www.spirehealthcare.com/edinburgh/.

16. Experts in Private Healthcare page on the SPIRE Edinburgh Hospitals website, 2013. Available at: http://www.spirehealth care.com/about-spire-healthcare/.

17. 'Entry and expansion case study 3: Edinburgh and the Lothians', Competition Commission, in 'Private healthcare market investi- gation', gov.uk, 4 April 2012.

18. S. Kenny, 'Rugby's "Bloodgate" scandal rolls on: Trainers "used razors to fake blood injuries" ', *Daily Mail*, 1 September 2009.

19. 'Harlequins' "Bloodgate" physio Steph Brennan struck off by Health Professions Council', telegraph.co.uk, 14 September 2010.

5. The Indemnity Question

1. 'All Blacks rate CSE "best" training facility', University of Edinburgh, 13 July 2012, ed.ac.uk.
2. 'Queen's Birthday honours: the full list', telegraph.co.uk, 12 June 2010.
3. 'James Robson awarded fellowship', Royal College of Surgeons of Edinburgh, 19 November 2010, rcsed.ac.uk.
4. SCOT consists of orthopaedic surgeons who are elected from the regions of Scotland and the clinical directors of the Scottish orthopaedic departments. *See* 'Scottish Committee for Orthopaedics and Trauma SCOT', Orthopaedic Seminar, orthopaedicseminar. com.
5. T. W. Hoskins, 'Prevention of neck injuries playing rugby', *Journal of Public Health*, 1987, 101(5) pp. 351–6. *See also* D. Du Toit, P. Olivier, L. Grenfell, B. Eksteen, 'Isokinetic neck strength norms for schoolboy rugby forwards', *South African Journal of Sports Medicine*, 2005, 17(1) pp. 19–26.
6. Letter from Bridget and Mike Broad to David Tolley, 22 November 2010.
7. Medical and Dental Defence Union of Scotland (MDDUS), Membership Agreement, 1 May 2010, mddus.com.
8. 'Aviva take over from Guinness to sponsor Premiership Rugby', *Daily Mail*, 7 July 2010.
9. 'Club accident insurance scheme', scottishrugby.org.
10. *See* 'Frequently Asked Questions – Insurance', Rugby Football Union website, rfu.com.
11. A. Samuels, 'Rugby injuries: liability of the club or college or school', *Medico-Legal Journal*, 2003, 71(2) pp. 85–6.
12. Ibid. *See also* R. Heywood, P. Charlish, 'Schoolmaster tackled hard over rugby incident', *Tort Law Review*, 2007, 15, shu.ac.uk.
13. Ibid.
14. Samuels, 'Rugby injuries'.
15. Ibid. *See also* Heywood et al., 'Schoolmaster tackled'.
16. Ibid.

17. S. Boufous, C. Finch, A. Bauman, 'Parental safety concerns – a barrier to sport and physical activity in children?', *Australian and New Zealand Journal of Public Health*, 2004, 28(5) pp. 482–6.

18. J. W. Orchard, C. Finch, 'Australia needs to follow New Zealand's lead on sports injuries', *Medical Journal of Australia*, 2002, 177(1) pp. 38–9.

19. 'What We Do' from the Hearts and Balls Charitable Trust website, heartsandballs.org.uk. *See also* The Rugby Football Union Injured Players Foundation website, rfuipf.org.uk.

6. The Cost of Injuries

1. The Scottish Parliament, Question SW3-39163: Ian Mckee, Lothians, Scottish National Party, date lodged 28 January 2011, answered 8 February 2011. Available at: http://www.scottish. parliament.uk/parliamentarybusiness/28877.aspx?SearchType= Advance&ReferenceNumbers=S3W-39163.

2. 'Royal Bank of Scotland – Principal Partner of Scottish Rugby', the Scottish Rugby Union official website, 2013, scottish rugby.org.

3. 'Scottish Rugby welcomes £1.4M investment', the Scottish Rugby Union official website, 2008, scottishrugby.org.

4. 'Scottish Rugby Honours Community Coach Graduates', the Scottish Rugby Union official website, 2007, scottishrugby.org.

5. Kirkwood et al., 'Preventing injury in children'. *See also* Kirkwood et al., 'Preventing injury in childhood'.

6. K. Khan, 'Crying wolf: when media reports distort research evidence', British Medical Journal Group Blogs, 7 September 2010, bmj.com.

7. Ibid.

8. Kirkwood et al., 'Preventing injury in childhood'. See also Allyson M. Pollock and Graham Kirkwood, 'Response to the Scottish Government's consultation on "Glasgow 2014 – Delivering a lasting legacy for Scotland"', The Centre for International Public Health Policy, May 2008, allysonpollock.com.

9. 'How does Sweden Compare', OECD Health Data 2005, oecd.org.
10. 'Safety Research and Development Programme', britisheventing. com, 2013.

7. Impossible to Ignore

1. M. McLaughlin, 'Glenalmond College axes rugby games over safety fear', *Scotsman*, 2 June 2013, scotsman.com.
2. http://www.espn.co.uk/scrum/rugby/story/190715.html
3. http://www.scotsman.com/sport/tom-english-rugby-concussion -rule-causes-alarm-1-2868497
4. 'MP Chris Bryant calls for parliamentary inquiry over concussion in sport', *Guardian*, 13 March 2014.
5. A. Kervin, 'Our concussion campaign is proud to win support from Parliament to Hollywood... as rugby leaders agree to review "five-minute rule" ', *Daily Mail*, 10 November 2013.

Part II. Hospital Pass

1. A. Junge, K. Cheung, T. Edwards, J. Dvořák, 'Injuries in youth amateur soccer and rugby players – comparison of incidence and characteristics', *British Journal of Sports Medicine*, 2004, 38(2) pp. 168–72. *See also* J. P. Sparks, 'Rugby football injuries, 1980– 1983', *British Journal of Sports Medicine*, 1985, 19(2) pp. 71–5. *See also* M. Nathan, R. Goedeke, T. D. Noakes, 'The incidence and nature of rugby injuries experienced at one school during the 1982 rugby season', *South African Medical Journal*, 1983, 64(4) pp. 132–7. *See also* C. E. Roux, R. Goedeke, G. R. Visser, W. A. van Zyl, T. D. Noakes, 'The epidemiology of school- boy rugby injuries', *South African Medical Journal*, 1987, 71(5) pp. 307–13.
2. 'The Role of Public Health in Injury Prevention 2007', World Health Organisation (WHO), who.int.
3. C. W. Fuller, M. G. Molloy, C. Bagate, R. Bahr, J. H. Brooks, H. Donson et al., 'Consensus statement on injury definitions and

data collection procedures for studies of injuries in rugby union', *British Journal of Sports Medicine*, 2007, 41(5) pp. 328–31.

4. Goldberg et al., 'Injury surveillance in young athletes'.

5. Junge et al., 'Injuries in youth amateur soccer and rugby players'.

6. Parekh et al., 'Communicating the risk of injury in schoolboy rugby'.

7. Fuller et al., 'Consensus statement on injury definitions'.

8. Ibid. A. Junge, K. Cheung, T. Edwards, J. Dvořák, 'Injuries in youth amateur soccer and rugby players – comparison of incidence and characteristics', *British Journal of Sports Medicine*, 2004, 38(2) pp. 168–72. *See also* J. P. Sparks, 'Rugby football injuries, 1980–1983', *British Journal of Sports Medicine*, 1985, 19(2) pp. 71–5. *See also* M. Nathan, R. Goedeke, T. D. Noakes, 'The incidence and nature of rugby injuries experienced at one school during the 1982 rugby season', *South African Medical Journal*, 1983, 64(4) pp. 132–7. *See also* C. E. Roux, R. Goedeke, G. R. Visser, W. A. van Zyl, T. D. Noakes, 'The epidemiology of schoolboy rugby injuries', *South African Medical Journal*, 1987, 71(5) pp. 307–13.

9. R. M. Davidson, M. Kennedy, J. Kennedy, G. Vanderfield, 'Casualty room presentations and schoolboy rugby union', *Medical Journal of Australia*, 1978, 1(5) pp. 247–9.

10. R. M. Davidson, 'Schoolboy Rugby injuries, 1969–1986', *Medical Journal of Australia*, 1987, 147(3) pp. 119–20.

11. R. M. Durie, A. D. Munroe, 'A Prospective Survey of Injuries in a New Zealand Schoolboy Rugby Population', *New Zealand Journal of Sports Medicine*, 2000, 28(4) pp. 84–91.

12. C. W. Fuller, M. G. Molloy, 'Epidemiological study of injuries in men's international under-20 rugby union tournaments', *Clinical Journal of Sport Medicine*, 2011, 21(4) pp. 356–8.

13. T. J. Gabbett, 'Incidence of injury in junior rugby league players over four competitive seasons', Journal of Science and Medicine in Sport, 2008, 11(3) pp. 323–8.

14. C. M. Haseler, M. R. Carmont, M. England, 'The epidemiology of injuries in English youth community rugby union', *British Journal of Sports Medicine*, 2010, 44(15) pp. 1093–9.

15. Junge et al., 'Injuries in youth amateur soccer and rugby players'.

16. A. S. McIntosh, P. McCrory, C. F. Finch, R. Wolfe, 'Head, face and neck injury in youth rugby: incidence and risk factors', *British Journal of Sports Medicine*, 2010, 44(3) pp. 188–93.

17. Nathan et al., 'The incidence and nature of rugby injuries'.

18. Nicol et al., 'Rugby union injuries in Scottish schools'.

19. D. S. Palmer-Green, K. A. Stokes, C. W. Fuller, M. England, S. P. Kemp, G. Trewartha, 'Match injuries in English youth academy and schools rugby union: an epidemiological study', *American Journal of Sports Medicine*, 2013, 41(4) pp. 749–55.

20. R.G. Pringle, 'Incidence of sporting injury in New Zealand youths aged 6–15 years', *British Journal of Sports Medicine*, 1998, 32(1) pp. 49–52.

21. Roux et al., 'The epidemiology of schoolboy rugby injuries'.

22. Sparks, 'Rugby football injuries, 1980–1983'.

23. Y. N. Bird, A. E. Waller, S. W. Marshall, J. C. Alsop, D. J. Chalmers, D. F. Gerrard, 'The New Zealand Rugby Injury and Performance Project: V. Epidemiology of a season of rugby injury', *British Journal of Sports Medicine*, 1998, 32(4) pp. 319–25.

24. C. L. Collins, L. J. Micheli, E. E. Yard, R. D. Comstock, 'Injuries sustained by high school rugby players in the United States, 2005–2006', *Archives of Pediatrics and Adolescent Medicine*, 2008, 162(1), 49–54.

25. S. W. Marshall, R. J. Spencer, 'Concussion in rugby: the hidden epidemic', *Journal of Athletic Training*, 2001, 36(3) pp. 334–8.

26. J. Usman, A. S. McIntosh, 'Upper limb injury in rugby union football: results of a cohort study', *British Journal of Sports Medicine*, 2013, 47(6) pp. 374–9.

27. Garraway et al., 'Impact of professionalism'.

28. A. J. Lee, 'Epidemiological comparison of injuries in school and senior club rugby', *British Journal of Sports Medicine*, 1996, 30(3) pp. 213–7.

29. Parekh et al., 'Communicating the risk of injury in schoolboy rugby'.

30. The incidence of injury per player-exposure is a population measure and does not convey the average probability of injury to an individual player during a rugby season. While incidence rates convey the harm to a population rising from a particular activity, perceptions of individual risk are more likely to be related to a person's individual risk probability.

31. See the brilliant work by Professor David Spiegelhalter on the public understanding of risk. His University of Cambridge profile is available at: http://www.csap.cam.ac.uk/network/david-spiegelhalter.

32. Parekh et al., 'Communicating the risk of injury in schoolboy rugby'.

33. It is true that the risks from surgery and sport are different in that the risk of sports injury increases with duration of play whereas the risk of complication during surgery does not necessarily increase with the duration of the operation. As such if there were fifteen individual injuries per 100 rugby players, it would be misleading to say to another player that irrespective of the amount of time that he plays, he has a 15 per cent chance of injury. However, the important point is that where there are risks of medical problems, the patient is able to interpret an average probability of it happening.

34. Samuels, 'Rugby injuries'.

35. Haseler et al., 'The epidemiology of injuries in English youth community rugby union'.

36. The formula for the probability of 'k' number of injuries in total time 't' hours of play is:

$$= \frac{(\lambda t)^k e^{-\lambda t}}{k!}, \text{ for } k = 0,1,2\ldots$$

P(k)

where:

λ = incidence of injuries per player-hour (so for 10.8 injuries per 1,000 player-hours λ = 0.0108)

t = time interval, hours (so for 15 matches, t = 15 × 70 minutes [or 60, depending on the length of the school game] = 17.5 hours)

e = base of the natural logarithm (e = 2.71828...)
k! = factorial of 'k'

37. Roux et al., 'The epidemiology of schoolboy rugby injuries'. *See also* Nicol et al., 'Rugby union injuries in Scottish schools'. *See also* Durie et al., 'A Prospective Survey of Injuries in a New Zealand Schoolboy Rugby Population'.

38. When only those injury incidence rates which are given in per 1,000 player-hours are pooled.

39. Fuller et al., 'Consensus statement on injury definitions'.

40. A. B. Spinks, R. J. McClure, 'Quantifying the risk of sports injury: a systematic review of activity-specific rates for children under 16 years of age', *British Journal of Sports Medicine*, 2007, 41(9) pp. 548–57.

41. Junge et al., 'Injuries in youth amateur soccer and rugby players'. *See also* A. D. Murray, I. R. Murray, J. Robson, 'Rugby Union: faster, higher, stronger: keeping an evolving sport safe', *British Journal of Sports Medicine*, 2012. *See also* S. J. Jones, R. A. Lyons, J. Sibert, R. Evans, S. R. Palmer, 'Changes in sports injuries to children between 1983 and 1998: comparison of case series', *Journal of Public Health*, 2001, 23(4) pp. 268–71. J. P. Sparks, 'Half a million hours of rugby football. The injuries', *British Journal of Sports Medicine*, 1981, 15(1) pp. 30–2. L. Abernethy, D. MacAuley, 'Impact of school sports injury', *British Journal of Sports Medicine*, 2003, 37(4) pp. 354–5. A. B. Spinks, A. K. Macpherson, C. Bain, Roderick J. McClure, 'Injury risk from popular childhood physical activities: results from an Australian primary school cohort', *Injury Prevention*, 2006, 12(6) pp. 390–4. *See also* D. Caine, C. Caine, N. Maffulli, 'Incidence and distribution of pediatric sport-related injuries', *Clinical Journal of Sport Medicine*, 2006, 16(6) pp. 500–13.

42. Abernethy et al., 'Impact of school sports injury'.

43. Jones et al., 'Changes in sports injuries to children between 1983 and 1998'.

44. 'Provisional monthly hospital episode statistics for admitted patient care, outpatients and accident and emergency data, April

2013 to November 2013', the Health and Social Care Information Centre (HSCIC) website, 19 February 2014.

45. Junge et al., 'Injuries in youth amateur soccer and rugby players'.

46. C. W. Fuller, 'Catastrophic injury in rugby union: is the level of risk acceptable', *Sports Medicine*, 2008, 38(12) pp. 975–86.

47. 'Principles and guidelines to assist HSE in its judgements that duty-holders have reduced risk as low as reasonably practicable', the Health and Safety Executive (HSE) website, 13 December 2001, hse.gov.uk.

48. Shelly et al., 'Spinal injuries in Irish rugby'. *See also* T. Kew, T. D. Noakes, A. N. Kettles, R. E. Goedeke, D. A. Newton, A. T. Scher, 'A retrospective study of spinal cord injuries in Cape Province rugby players, 1963–1989. Incidence, mechanisms and prevention', *South African Medical Journal*, 1991, 80(3) pp. 127–33. S. Gianotti, P. A. Hume, W. G. Hopkins, J. Harawira, R. Truman, 'Interim evaluation of the effect of a new scrum law on neck and back injuries in rugby union', *British Journal of Sports Medicine*, 2008, 42(6) pp. 427–30.

49. B. Bowley, 'Constructions of masculinity in young sporty boys: the case of KwaZulu-Natal Preparatory School's first rugby team', Masters thesis, University of KwaZulu-Natal, 2006.

50. K. Liston, D. Reacher, A. Smith, I. Waddington, 'Managing pain and injury in non-elite rugby union and rugby league: a case of players at a British university', *Sport in Society: Cultures, Commerce, Media, Politics*, 2006, 9(3) pp. 388–402.

51. Garraway et al., 'Impact of professionalism'. *See also* J. H. Brooks, S. P. Kemp, 'Recent trends in rugby union injuries', *Clinical Sports Medicine*, 2008, 27(1) pp. 51–73, vii–viii.

52. 'England Professional Rugby Injury Surveillance Project, 2011–2012 Season Report', Rugby Football Union (RFU), March 2013, rfu.com.

53. Sparks, 'Rugby football injuries, 1980–1983'. *See also* Nathan et al., 'The incidence and nature of rugby injuries'; Durie et al., 'A Prospective Survey of Injuries in a New Zealand Schoolboy Rugby Population'; Gabbett, 'Incidence of injury in junior rugby

league players over four competitive seasons'; Haseler et al., 'The epidemiology of injuries in English youth community rugby union'; Junge et al., 'Injuries in youth amateur soccer and rugby players'; McIntosh et al., 'Head, face and neck injury in youth rugby'; Nicol et al., 'Rugby union injuries in Scottish schools'; Palmer-Green et al., 'Match injuries in English youth academy and schools rugby union'; Roux et al., 'The epidemiology of schoolboy rugby injuries'; Bird et al., 'The New Zealand Rugby Injury and Performance Project'; Collins et al., 'Injuries sustained by high school rugby players in the United States, 2005–2006'; Marshall et al., 'Concussion in rugby: the hidden epidemic'; Lee, 'Epidemiological comparison of injuries in school and senior club rugby'; Sparks, 'Half a million hours of rugby football'; Finch et al., 'Sport and active recreation injuries in Australia: Evidence from emergency department presentations', *British Journal of Sports Medicine*, 1998, 32(3) pp. 220–5; Sugerman, 'Injuries in an Australian schools rugby union season'; E. R. Lewis, K. P. George, 'An initial investigation of injuries in women, men and youths playing Rugby Union football at the same club', *Sports Excercise and Injury*, 1996, 2(4) pp. 186–91; A. B. Shuttleworth-Edwards, T. D. Noakes, S. E. Radloff, V. J. Whitefield, S. B. Clark, C. O. Roberts et al., 'The comparative incidence of reported concussions presenting for follow-up management in South African Rugby Union', *Clinical Journal of Sports Medicine*, 2008, 18(5) pp. 403–9; P. A. H. Upton, C. E. Roux, T. D. Noakes, 'Inadequate pre-season preparation of schoolboy rugby players – A survey of players at 25 Cape Province high schools', *South African Medical Journal*, 1996, 86(5) pp. 531–3; J. F. Baker, B. M. Devitt, J. Green, C. McCarthy, 'Concussion among under-20 rugby union players in Ireland: incidence, attitudes and knowledge', *Irish Journal of Medical Sciences*, 2013, 182(1) pp. 121–5.

54. Sparks, 'Rugby football injuries, 1980–1983'. See also Durie et al., 'A Prospective Survey of Injuries in a New Zealand Schoolboy Rugby Population'. *See also* Sparks, 'Half a million hours of rugby football'. *See also* MacQueen et al., 'Injury trends and prevention

in rugby union football'. See also S. Sugerman, 'Injuries in an Australian schools rugby union season', *Australian Journal of Sports Medicine and Exercise Science*, 1983, 15(1) pp. 5–18.

55. Sparks, 'Rugby football injuries, 1980–1983'. *See also* Roux et al., 'The epidemiology of schoolboy rugby injuries'; Davidson, 'Schoolboy Rugby injuries, 1969–1986'; Haseler et al., 'The epidemiology of injuries in English youth community rugby union'; McIntosh et al., 'Head, face and neck injury in youth rugby'; Nicol et al., 'Rugby union injuries in Scottish schools'; Collins et al., 'Injuries sustained by high school rugby players in the United States, 2005–2006'; MacQueen et al., 'Injury trends and prevention in rugby union football'; A. S. McIntosh, 'Rugby injuries', *Medicine and Sport Science*, 2005, 49, pp. 120–39.

56. M. R. Proctor, R. C. Cantu, 'Head and neck injuries in young athletes', *Clinical Sports Medicine*, 2000, 19(4) pp. 693–715.

57. Junge et al., 'Injuries in youth amateur soccer and rugby players'. *See also* Palmer-Green et al., 'Match injuries in English youth academy and schools rugby union'; Brooks et al., 'Recent trends in rugby union injuries'.

58. Haseler et al., 'The epidemiology of injuries in English youth community rugby union'. *See also* Nicol et al., 'Rugby union injuries in Scottish schools'; Collins et al., 'Injuries sustained by high school rugby players in the United States, 2005–2006'; Sugerman, 'Injuries in an Australian schools rugby union season'.

59. P. McCrory, W. H. Meeuwisse, M. Aubry, B. Cantu, J. Dvořák, R. J. Echemendia, L. Engebretsen, K. Johnston, J. S. Kutcher, M. Raftery, A. Sills, B. W. Benson, G. A. Davis, R. Ellenbogan, K. Guskiewicz, S. A. Herring, G. L. Iverson, B. D. Jordan, J. Kissick, M. McCrea, A. S. McIntosh, D. Maddocks, M. Makdissi, L. Purcell, M. Putukian, K. Schneider, C. H. Tator, M. Turner, 'Consensus statement on concussion in sport: the 4th International Conference on Concussion in Sport held in Zurich, November 2012', *Journal of the American College of Surgeons*, 2013, 216(5) pp. e55–71.

60. K. G. Harmon, J. A. Drezner, M. Gammons, K. M. Guskiewicz,

M. Halstead, S. A. Herring et al., 'American Medical Society for Sports Medicine position statement: concussion in sport', *British Journal of Sports Medicine*, 2013, 47(1) pp. 15–26.

61. Ibid.

62. Ibid. *See also* McCrory et al.,'Consensus statement on concussion in sport'; R. Graham, F. P. Rivara, M. A. Ford, C. M. Spicer, and editors, *Sports-Related Concussions in Youth: Improving the Science, Changing the Culture*, National Academic Press (US), 2014.

63. Graham et al., *Sports-Related Concussions in Youth. See also* Harmon et al., 'American Medical Society for Sports Medicine position statement'.

64. S. P. Broglio, T. W. Puetz, 'The effect of sport concussion on neurocognitive function, self-report symptoms and postural control: a meta-analysis', *British Journal of Sports Medicine*, 2008, 38(1), 53–67.

65. T. W. Teasdale, A. W. Engberg, L. G. Holte, 'Double concussions and cognitive dysfunction: A population study of young men', *Brain Impairment*, 2012, 13 pp. 197–202.

66. T. W. Teasdale, A. J. Frosig, 'Cognitive ability and educational level in relation to concussion: a population study of young men', *BMJ Open*, 9 Mary 2013.

67. Graham et al., *Sports-Related Concussions in Youth*.

68. A. Gardner, E. A. Shores, J. Batchelor, 'Reduced processing speed in rugby union players reporting three or more previous concussions', *Archives of Clinical Neuropsychology*, 2010, 25(3) pp.174–81

69. R. S. Moser, P. Schatz, B. D. Jordan, 'Prolonged effects of concussion in high school athletes', *Neurosurgery*, 2005, 57(2) pp. 300–6; discussion 300–6.

70. K. M. Guskiewicz, S. W. Marshall, J. Bailes, M. McCrea, R. C. Cantu, C. Randolph, B. D. Jordan, 'Association between recurrent concussion and late-life cognitive impairment in retired professional football players', *Neurosurgery*, 2005, 57(4) pp. 719-26; discussion 719–26.

71. L. De Beaumont, H. Théoret, D. Mongeon, J. Messier, S. Leclerc,

S. Tremblay, D. Ellemberg, M. Lassonde, 'Brain function decline in healthy retired athletes who sustained their last sports concussion in early adulthood', *Brain*, 132(3) pp. 695–708. *See also* S. Tremblay, L. De Beaumont, L. C. Henry, Y. Boulanger, A. C. Evans, P. Bourgouin, J. Poirier, H. Théoret, M. Lassonde, 'Sports concussions and aging: a neuroimaging investigation', *Cerebral Cortex*, 2013, 23(5) pp. 1159–66.

72. N. Gosselin, C. Bottari, J. Chen, S. Christina Huntgeburth, L. De Beaumont, M. Petrides, B. Cheung, A. Ptito, 'Evaluating the cognitive consequences of mild traumatic brain injury and concussion by using electrophysiology', *Neurosurgical Focus*, 2012, 33(6) pp. E7: 1–7.

73. J. M. Ling, S. Klimaj, T. Toulouse, A. R. Mayer, 'A prospective study of gray matter abnormalities in mild traumatic brain injury', *Neurology*, 2013, 81(24) pp. 2121–7.

74. N. Marchi, J. J. Bazarian, V. Puvenna, M. Janigro, C. Ghosh, J. Zhong, T. Zhu, E. Blackman, D. Stewart, J. Ellis, R. Butler, D. Janigro, 'Consequences of repeated blood-brain barrier disruption in football players', *PLoS ONE*, 2013, 8(3) e56805, 10.1371/journal.pone.0056805.

75. Ibid. *See also* B. Roehr, 'Grappling with concussion: discovery, policy, and practice', *British Medical Journal*, 2013, 346 f1693.

76. R. A. Stern, D. O. Riley, D. H. Daneshvar, C. J. Nowinski, R. C. Cantu, A. C. McKee, 'Long-term consequences of repetitive brain trauma: chronic traumatic encephalopathy', *PM&R: The Journal of Injury, Function, and Rehabilitation*, 2011, 3(10, Supplement 2) pp. S460–7. *See also* McCrory et al., 'Consensus statement on concussion in sport'. *See also* Iverson G. L. 'Chronic traumatic encephalopathy and risk of suicide in former athletes'. *British Journal of Sports Medicine* 2014, 48(2):162–5. And Dick B. 'Dr Michael Grey voices fears over concussion in rugby'. *Birmingham Mail, available at*: http://www.birminghammail.co.uk/sport/rugby/special-feature-university-birminghams-dr-6232894.

77. Stern et al., 'Long-term consequences of repetitive brain trauma'. *See also* 'Rugby "linked to early onset dementia" ', BBC.co.uk,

3 August 2013. *See also* Lawton G. 'Rugby players warned of long-term brain injury risks'. *New Scientist*, 12 March 2014.

78. Stern et al., 'Long-term consequences of repetitive brain trauma'. *See also* Gardner et al., 'Reduced processing speed in rugby union players'. *See also* A. Gardner, G. L. Iverson, P. McCrory, 'Chronic traumatic encephalopathy in sport: a systematic review', *British Journal of Sports Medicine* 2014; 48(2), pp. 84–90.

79. Guskiewicz et al., 'Association between recurrent concussion and late-life cognitive impairment in retired professional football players'.

80. J. J. Bazarian, I. Cernak, L. Noble-Haeusslein, S. Potolicchio, N. Temkin, 'Long-term neurologic outcomes after traumatic brain injury', *Journal of Head Trauma Rehabilitation*, 2009, 24(6) pp. 439–51.

81. S. Jafari, M. Etminan, F. Aminzadeh, A. Samii, 'Head injury and risk of Parkinson disease: a systematic review and meta-analysis', *Movement Disorders*, 2013, 28(9) pp. 1222–9.

82. Graham et al., *Sports-Related Concussions in Youth*. *See also* McCrory et al.,'Consensus statement on concussion in sport'; Harmon et al., 'American Medical Society for Sports Medicine position statement'; H. Zetterberg, D. H. Smith, K. Blennow, 'Biomarkers of mild traumatic brain injury in cerebrospinal fluid and blood', *Nature Reviews Neurology*, 2013, 9(4) pp. 201–10; G. A. Davis, L. K. Purcell, 'The evaluation and management of acute concussion differs in young children', *British Journal of Sports Medicine*, 2014, 48(2) pp. 98–101; American Academy of Neurology, Position and Policy Documents, Sports Concussion, 2013, aan.com.

83. *See also* Harmon et al., 'American Medical Society for Sports Medicine position statement'; Mark E. Halstead, Kevin D. Walter and the Council on Sports Medicine and Fitness, 'Clinical report – Sport-Related Concussion in Children and Adolescents', *Pediatrics*, 2010, 126(3) pp. 597–615; *Position Statement: Sports Concussion*, American Academy of Neurology, 2013, aan.com.

84. E. E. Yard, R. D. Comstock, 'Injuries sustained by rugby players

presenting to United States emergency departments, 1978 through 2004', *Journal of Athletic Training*, 2006, 41(3) pp. 325–31.

85. S. L. Zuckerman, Y. M. Lee, M. J. Odom, G. S. Solomon, J. A. Forbes, A. K. Sills, 'Recovery from sports-related concussion: Days to return to neurocognitive baseline in adolescents versus young adults', *Surgical Neurology International*, 2012, 3 p. 130.

86. Harmon et al., 'American Medical Society for Sports Medicine position statement'. *See also* Graham et al., *Sports-Related Concussions in Youth*.

87. Harmon et al., 'American Medical Society for Sports Medicine position statement'. *See also* S. J. Hollis, M. R. Stevenson, A. S. McIntosh, E. A. Shores, M. W. Collins, C. B. Taylor, 'Incidence, risk, and protective factors of mild traumatic brain injury in a cohort of Australian nonprofessional male rugby players', *American Journal of Sports Medicine*, 2009, 37(12) pp. 2328–33.

88. P. McCrory, W. H. Meeuwisse, R. J. Echemendia, G. L. Iverson, J. Dvořák, J. S. Kutcher, 'What is the lowest threshold to make a diagnosis of concussion?', *British Journal of Sports Medicine*, 2013, 47(5) pp. 268–71.

89. McCrory et al.,'Consensus statement on concussion in sport'. *See also* S. Alla, S. J. Sullivan, L. Hale, P. McCrory, 'Self-report scales/checklists for the measurement of concussion symptoms: a systematic review', *British Journal of Sports Medicine*, 2009, 43(Supplement 1) pp. i3–12.

90. Graham et al., *Sports-Related Concussions in Youth*.

91. J. S. Kutcher, P. McCrory, G. Davis, A. Ptito, W. H. Meeuwisse, S. P. Broglio, 'What evidence exists for new strategies or technologies in the diagnosis of sports concussion and assessment of recovery?' *British Journal of Sports Medicine*, 2013, 47(5) pp. 299–303.

92. C. C. Giza, J. S. Kutcher, S. Ashwal, J. Barth, T. S. Getchius, G. A. Gioia, G. S. Gronseth, K. Guskiewicz, S. Mandel, G. Manley, D. B. McKeag, D. J. Thurman, R. Zafonte, 'Summary of evidence-based guideline update: evaluation and management of concussion in sports: report of the Guideline Development Subcommittee of

the American Academy of Neurology', *Neurology*, 2013, 80(24) pp. 2250–7.

93. McCrory et al.,'Consensus statement on concussion in sport'.

94. Alla et al., 'Self-report scales/checklists for the measurement of concussion symptoms'.

95. B. D. Jordan, 'The clinical spectrum of sport-related traumatic brain injury', *Nature Reviews Neurology*, 2013, 9(4) pp. 222–30.

96. Proctor et al., 'Head and neck injuries in young athletes'.

97. Jordan, 'The clinical spectrum of sport-related traumatic brain injury'. *See also* 'Patient Information: Concussion', from the American Association of Neurological Surgeons (AANS) website, updated December 2011, aans.org.

98. Ibid.

99. Fuller et al., 'Epidemiological study of injuries in men's international under-20 rugby union tournaments'.

100. Haseler et al., 'The epidemiology of injuries in English youth community rugby union'.

101. Usman et al., 'Upper limb injury in rugby union football'.

102. Sparks, 'Rugby football injuries, 1980–1983'.

103. Nicol et al., 'Rugby union injuries in Scottish schools'.

104. Palmer-Green et al., 'Match injuries in English youth academy and schools rugby union'.

105. Nicol et al., 'Rugby union injuries in Scottish schools'.

106. Ibid.

107. Lee, 'Epidemiological comparison of injuries in school and senior club rugby'.

108. J. P. Sparks, 'Rugby football injuries, 1980–1983', *British Journal of Sports Medicine*, 1985, 19(2) pp. 71–5. *See also* M. Nathan, R. Goedeke, T. D. Noakes, 'The incidence and nature of rugby injuries experienced at one school during the 1982 rugby season', *South African Medical Journal*, 1983, 64(4) pp. 132–7. R. M. Durie, A. D. Munroe, 'A prospective survey of injuries in a New Zealand schoolboy rugby population', *New Zealand Journal of Sports Medicine*, 2000, 28(4) pp. 84–91. C. W. Fuller, M. G. Molloy, M. Marsalli, 'Epidemiological study of injuries

in men's international under-20 rugby union tournaments', *Clinical Journal of Sports Medicine*, 2011, 21(4) pp. 356–8. A. S. McIntosh, P. McCrory, C.F. Finch, R. Wolfe, 'Head, face and neck injury in youth rugby: incidence and risk factors', *British Journal of Sports Medicine*, 2010, 44(3) pp. 188–93. A. Nicol, A. M. Pollock, G. Kirkwood, N. Parekh, J. Robson, 'Rugby union injuries in Scottish schools', *Journal of Public Health*, Oxford: 2011, 33(2) pp. 256–61. D. S. Palmer-Green, K. A. Stokes, C. W. Fuller, M. England, S.P. Kemp, G. Trewartha, 'Match injuries in English youth academy and schools rugby union: an epidemiological study', *American Journal of Sports Medicine*, 2013, 41(4) pp. 749–55. C. E. Roux, R. Goedeke, G. R. Visser, W. A. van Zyl, T.D. Noakes, 'The epidemiology of schoolboy rugby injuries', *South African Medical Journal*, 1987, 71(5) pp. 307–13. C. L. Collins, L. J. Micheli, E. E. Yard, R. D. Comstock, 'Injuries sustained by high school rugby players in the United States, 2005–2006', *Archives of Pediatrics and Adolescent Medicine*, 2008, 162(1), 49–54. A. J. Lee, 'Epidemiological comparison of injuries in school and senior club rugby', *British Journal of Sports Medicine*, 1996, 30(3) pp. 213–7.

109. Palmer-Green et al., 'Match injuries in English youth academy and schools rugby union'. *See also* Brooks et al., 'Recent trends in rugby union injuries'.

110. W. M. Garraway, A. J. Lee, D. A. Macleod, J. W. Telfer, I. J. Deary, G. D. Murray, 'Factors influencing tackle injuries in rugby union football', *British Journal of Sports Medicine*, 1999, 33(1) pp. 37–41.

111. Sugerman, 'Injuries in an Australian schools rugby union season'.

112. Garraway et al., 'Factors influencing tackle injuries in rugby union football'.

113. Ibid.

114. S. Hendricks, E. Jordaan, M. Lambert, 'Attitude and behaviour of junior rugby union players towards tackling during training and match play', *Safety Science*, February 2012, 50(2), pp. 266–84.

115. Garraway et al., 'Factors influencing tackle injuries in rugby union football'.

116. Silver, 'The impact of the 21st century on rugby injuries'. *See also* E. Preatoni, K. A. Stokes, M. E. England, G. Trewartha, 'The influence of playing level on the biomechanical demands experienced by rugby union forwards during machine scrummaging', *Scandinavian Journal of Medicine and Science in Sports*, 2013, 23(3) pp. e178–84.

117. Roux et al., 'The epidemiology of schoolboy rugby injuries'. *See also* Palmer-Green et al., 'Match injuries in English youth academy and schools rugby union'; Durie et al., 'A Prospective Survey of Injuries in a New Zealand Schoolboy Rugby Population'; McIntosh, 'Rugby injuries'; A. J. Lee, W. M. Garraway, W. Hepburn, R. Laidlaw, 'Influence of rugby injuries on players' subsequent health and lifestyle: beginning a long term follow up', *British Journal of Sports Medicine*, 2001 35(1) pp. 38–42.

118. MacLean et al., 'Serious neck injuries in U19 rugby union players'. *See also* C. W. Fuller, J. H. Brooks, R. J. Cancea, J. Hall, S. P. Kemp, 'Contact events in rugby union and their propensity to cause injury', *British Journal of Sports Medicine*, 2007, 41(12) pp. 862–7; discussion 7; James Craig Brown, Mike I. Lambert, Evert Verhagen, Clint Readhead, Willem van Mechelen, Wayne Viljoen, 'The incidence of rugby-related catastrophic injuries (including cardiac events) in South Africa from 2008 to 2011: a cohort study', *BMJ Open*, 2013, 3(2) 10.1136/bmjopen-2012-002475.

119. Silver, 'The impact of the 21st century on rugby injuries'. *See also* G. J. Browne, 'Cervical spinal injury in children's community rugby football', *British Journal of Sports Medicine*, 2006, 40(1) pp. 68–71.

120. Proctor et al., 'Head and neck injuries in young athletes'.

121. Gianotti et al., 'Interim evaluation of the effect of a new scrum law on neck and back injuries in rugby union'.

122. MacLean et al., 'Serious neck injuries in U19 rugby union players'.

123. Ibid.

124. Preatoni et al., 'The influence of playing level on the

biomechanical demands experienced by rugby union forwards during machine scrummaging'.

125. MacQueen et al., 'Injury trends and prevention in rugby union football'. *See also* Preatoni et al., 'The influence of playing level on the biomechanical demands experienced by rugby union forwards during machine scrummaging'.

126. F. P. Secin, E. J. Poggi, F. Luzuriaga, H. A. Laffaye, 'Disabling injuries of the cervical spine in Argentine rugby over the last 20 years', *British Journal of Sports Medicine*, 1999, 33(1) pp. 33–6.

127. Brooks et al., 'Recent trends in rugby union injuries'.

128. M. S. Swain, R. P. Lystad, H. Pollard, R. Bonello, 'Incidence and severity of neck injury in Rugby Union: a systematic review', *Journal of Science and Medicine in Sport*, 2011, 14(5) pp. 383–9.

129. Brooks et al., 'Recent trends in rugby union injuries'. *See also* MacQueen et al., 'Injury trends and prevention in rugby union football'; Swain et al., 'Incidence and severity of neck injury in Rugby Union'.

130. Sparks, 'Rugby football injuries, 1980–1983'. *See also* Nathan et al., 'The incidence and nature of rugby injuries'; Davidson, 'Schoolboy Rugby injuries, 1969–1986'; Durie et al., 'A prospective survey of injuries in a New Zealand schoolboy rugby population'; Roux et al., 'The epidemiology of schoolboy rugby injuries'; Sugerman, 'Injuries in an Australian schools rugby union season'; A. McManus and D. S. Cross, 'Incidence of injury in elite junior Rugby Union: a prospective descriptive study', *Journal of Science and Medicine in Sport*, 2004, 7(4) pp. 438–45.

131. Craig Brown et al., 'The incidence of rugby-related catastrophic injuries (including cardiac events) in South Africa from 2008 to 2011'.

132. Ibid.

133. M. Nathan, R. Goedeke, T. D. Noakes, 'The incidence and nature of rugby injuries experienced at one school during the 1982 rugby season', *South African Medical Journal*, 1983, 64(4) pp. 132–7; Mcintosh et al., 'Head face and neck injury in youth rugby'.

134. C. Bleakley, M. Tully, S. O'Connor, 'Epidemiology of adolescent rugby injuries: a systematic review', *Journal of Athletic Training*, 2011, 46(5) pp. 555–65.

135. Brooks et al., 'Recent trends in rugby union injuries'.

136. Ibid.

137. Bleakley et al., 'Epidemiology of adolescent rugby injuries'.

138. P. A. H. Upton, C. E. Roux, T. D. Noakes, 'Inadequate pre-season preparation of schoolboy rugby players – a survey of players at 25 Cape Province high schools', *South African Medical Journal*, 1996, 86(5) pp. 531–3.

139. S. M. Gianotti, K. L. Quarrie, P. A. Hume, 'Evaluation of RugbySmart: a rugby union community injury prevention programme', *Journal of Science and Medicine in Sport*, 2009, 12(3) pp. 371–5.

140. K. L. Quarrie, S. M. Gianotti, D. J. Chalmers, W. G. Hopkins, 'An evaluation of mouthguard requirements and dental injuries in New Zealand rugby union', *British Journal of Sports Medicine*, 2005, 39(9) pp. 650–1.

141. Gianotti et al., 'Evaluation of RugbySmart'.

142. S. W. Marshall, D. P. Loomis, A. E. Waller, D. J. Chalmers, Y. N. Bird, K. L. Quarrie et al., 'Evaluation of protective equipment for prevention of injuries in rugby union', *International Journal of Epidemiology*, 2005, 34(1) pp. 113–8.

143. McCrory et al., 'Consensus statement on concussion in sport'. *See also* Marshall et al., 'Evaluation of protective equipment for prevention of injuries in rugby union'; N. Upson, 'Mouthguards, an evaluation of two types for rugby players', *British Journal of Sports Medicine*, 1985, 19(2) pp. 89–92.

144. Giza et al., 'Summary of evidence-based guideline update'. *See also* B. W. Benson, G. M. Hamilton, W. H. Meeuwisse, P. McCrory, J. Dvořák, 'Is protective equipment useful in preventing concussion? A systematic review of the literature', *British Journal of Sports Medicine*, 2009, 43(Suppl 1) pp. i56–67.

145. C. Finch, R. Braham, A. McIntosh, P. McCrory, R. Wolfe, 'Should football players wear custom fitted mouthguards? Results from a

group randomised controlled trial', *Injury Prevention*, 2005, 11(4) pp. 242–6.

146. Quarrie et al., 'An evaluation of mouthguard requirements and dental injuries in New Zealand rugby union'.

147. Player Health: Frequently Asked Questions: Rugby Football Union (RFU), 2013, rfu.com.

148. 'Othodontic and Contact sports', British Orthodontic Society (BOS), 2013, bos.org.uk. Available at: http://www.bos.org.uk/schools/orthodontic-contact-sports.

149. Nicol et al., 'Rugby union injuries in Scottish schools'.

150. M. O'Malley, D. S. Evans, A. Hewson, J. Owens, 'Mouthguard use and dental injury in sport: a questionnaire study of national school children in the west of Ireland', *Journal of the Irish Dental Association*, 2012, 58(4) pp. 205–11.

151. R. R. Navarro, 'Protective equipment and the prevention of concussion – what is the evidence?' *Current Sports Medicine Reports*, 2011, 10(1) pp. 27–31.

152. C. F. Finch, A. S. McIntosh, P. McCrory, 'What do under-15-year-old schoolboy rugby union players think about protective headgear?' *British Journal of Sports Medicine*, 2001, 35(2) pp. 89–94.

153. Lee et al., 'Influence of rugby injuries on players' subsequent health and lifestyle'.

154. Gianotti et al., 'Evaluation of RugbySmart'.

155. 'The Private Sector as Service Provider and its Role in Implementing Child Rights', Office of the High Commissioner for Human Rights (OHCHR), 2002, ohchr.org.

156. 'Convention on the rights of the child', Office of the High Commissioner for Human Rights (OHCHR), 2 September, 1990, ohchr.org.

157. Ibid.

158. 'The right of the child to freedom from all forms of violence', from the United Nations Convention on the Rights of the Child (CRC), 18 April 2011, unicef.org.

159. The Convention on the Rights of the Child, Protection rights: keeping safe from harm (article 4), UNICEF, 2013, unicef.org.

160. General comment No. 17 (2013) on the right of the child to rest, leisure, play, recreational activities, cultural life and the arts (art. 31), The Convention on the rights of the child, 2013, unicef.org.

161. 'Woodland v Essex County Council', 23 October 2013, (file number: UKSC 66, UKSC 2012/0093), supremecourt.uk. Available at: http://www.7br.co.uk/uploads/uksc-2012-0093-judgment.pdf.

162. Heywood et al., 'Schoolmaster tackled'.

163. Kristal L. Tomei, Christopher Doe, Charles J. Prestigiacomo and Chirag D. Gandhi, 'Comparative analysis of state-level concussion legislation and review of current practices in concussion', *Neurosurgical Focus*, 2012, 33(6) p. E11.

164. McCrory et al.,'Consensus statement on concussion in sport'.

165. Adapted from Kirkwood et al., 'Preventing injury in children'.

166. Goldberg et al., 'Injury surveillance in young athletes'. *See also* E. P. Cassell, C. P. Finch, V. Z. Stathakis, 'Epidemiology of medically treated sport and active recreation injuries in the Latrobe Valley, Victoria, Australia', *British Journal of Sports Medicine* 2003; 37 (5):405–9. J. P. Nicholl, P. Coleman, B. T. Williams, 'Pilot study of the epidemiology of sports injuries and exercise-related morbidity', *British Journal of Sports Medicine*, 1991, 25 (1): pp. 61–6

167. Nicol et al., 'Rugby union injuries in Scottish schools'.

168. Goldberg et al., 'Injury surveillance in young athletes'.

169. Cusimano et al., 'Mechanisms of team-sport-related brain injuries in children 5 to 19 years old'. *See also* R. Dick, J. Agel, S. W. Marshall, 'National Collegiate Athletic Association Injury Surveillance System commentaries: introduction and methods', *Journal of Athletic Training*, 2007, 42(2) pp. 173–82.

Part III. Peroration

1. 'Neglect of sports medicine', *British Medical Journal*, 9 July 1977.

2. 'Rugby injuries to the cervical cord', *British Medical Journal*, 18 June 1977.

3. R. C. Schneider, *Head and Neck Injuries in Football*, p. 126, Baltimore, Williams and Wilkins, 1973.

4. A. T. Scher, *South African Medical Journal*, 1977, 51, p. 473.

5. A sample of the correspondence can be read on the *British Journal of Sports Medicine* website. 'Neglect of Sports Medicine', *British Journal of Sports Medicine*, 1977, 11, pp. 150–2.

Appendix 1

1. Parekh et al., 'Communicating the risk of injury in schoolboy rugby'.

2. Nathan et al., 'The incidence and nature of rugby injuries'.

3. Sparks, 'Rugby football injuries, 1980–1983'.

4. Davidson, 'Schoolboy rugby injuries, 1969–1986'.

5. Roux et al., 'The epidemiology of schoolboy rugby injuries'.

6. Durie et al., 'A prospective survey of injuries in a New Zealand schoolboy rugby population'.

7. Junge et al., 'Injuries in youth amateur soccer and rugby players'.

8. McIntosh, 'Rugby injuries'.

9. McIntosh et al., 'Head, face and neck injury in youth rugby'.

10. Haseler et al., 'The epidemiology of injuries in English youth community rugby union'.

11. Nicol et al., 'Rugby union injuries in Scottish schools'.

Appendix 2

1. J. F. Baker, B. M. Devitt, J. Green, C. Mccarthy, 'Concussion among under-20 rugby union players in Ireland: Incidence, attitudes and knowledge', *Irish Journal of Medical Sciences*, 2013, 182 pp. 121–5.

2. C. L. Collins, L. J. Micheli, E. E. Yard, R. D. Comstock, 'Injuries sustained by high school rugby players in the United States, 2005–2006', *Archives of Pediatrics and Adolescent Medicine*, 2008, 162 pp. 49–54.

3. R. M. Durie, A. D. Munroe, 'A prospective survey of injuries in a

New Zealand schoolboy rugby population', *New Zealand Journal of Sports Medicine*, 2000, 28 pp. 84–91.

4. C. W. Fuller, M. G. Molloy, 'Epidemiological study of injuries in men's international under-20 rugby union tournaments', *Clinical Journal of Sport Medicine*, 2011, 21 pp. 356–8.

5. T. J. Gabbett, 'Incidence of injury in junior rugby league players over four competitive seasons', *Journal of Science and Medicine in Sport*, 2008, 11 pp. 323–8.

6. C. M. Haseler, M. R. Carmont, M. England, 'The epidemiology of injuries in English youth community rugby union', *British Journal of Sports Medicine*, 2010, 44 pp. 1093–9.

7. A. Junge, K. Cheung, T. Edwards, J. Dvorak, 'Injuries in youth amateur soccer and rugby players – Comparison of incidence and characteristics', *British Journal of Sports Medicine*, 2004, 38 pp. 168–72.

8. D. King, 'Incidence of injuries in the 2005 New Zealand national junior rugby league competition', *New Zealand Journal of Sports Medicine*, 2006, 34 pp. 21–7.

9. D. King, Gissane, C., Clark, T. 'Concussion in amateur rugby league players in New Zealand: A review of player concussion history', *New Zealand Journal of Sports Medicine*, 40, pp. 64–9.

10. A. J. Lee, 'Epidemiological comparison of injuries in school and senior club rugby', *British Journal of Sports Medicine*, 1996, 30 pp. 213–7.

11. E. R. Lewis, K. P. George, 'An initial investigation of injuries in women, men and youths playing rugby union football at the same club', *Sports Exercise and Injury*, 1996, 2 pp. 186–91.

12. S. W. Marshall, R. J. Spencer, 'Concussion in rugby: the hidden epidemic', *Journal of Athletic Training*, 2001, 36 pp. 334–8.

13. A. S. Mcintosh, P. Mccrory, C. F. Finch, R. Wolfe, 'Head, face and neck injury in youth rugby: Incidence and risk factors', *British Journal of Sports Medicine*, 2010, 44 pp. 188–93.

14. M. Nathan, R. Goedeke, T. D. Noakes, 'The incidence and nature of rugby injuries experienced at one school during the 1982 rugby season', *South African Medical Journal*, 1983, 64 pp. 132–7.

15. A. Nicol, A. Pollock, G. Kirkwood, N. Parekh, J. Robson, 'Rugby union injuries in Scottish schools', *Journal of Public Health*, 2011, 33 pp. 256–61.

16. C. E. Roux, R. Goedeke, G. R. Visser, 'The epidemiology of schoolboy rugby injuries', *South African Medical Journal*, 1987, 71 pp. 307–13.

17. A. B. Shuttleworth-Edwards, T. D. Noakes, S. E. Radloff, V. J. Whitefield, S. B. Clark, C. O. Roberts, F. B. Essack, D. Zoccola, M. J. Boulind, S. E. Case, I. P. Smith, J. L. Mitchell, 'The comparative incidence of reported concussions presenting for follow-up management in South African rugby union', *Clinical Journal of Sport Medicine*, 2008, 18 pp. 403–9.

18. J. P. Sparks, 'Half a million hours of rugby football. The injuries', *British Journal of Sports Medicine*, 1981, 15 pp. 30–2.

19. J. P. Sparks, 'Rugby football injuries, 1980–1983', *British Journal of Sports Medicine*, 1985, 19 pp. 71–5.

20. S. Sugerman, 'Injuries in an Australian schools rugby union season', *Australian Journal of Sports Medicine and Exercise Science*, 1983, 15 pp. 5–18.

21. P. A. H. Upton, C. E. Roux, T. D. Noakes, 'Inadequate pre-season preparation of schoolboy rugby players – A survey of players at 25 Cape Province high schools', *South African Medical Journal*, 1996, 86 pp. 531–3.

22. A. W. S. Watson, 'Injuries in schoolboy players of basketball, field-hockey, hurling, Gaelic football, rugby and soccer', *New Zealand Journal of Sports Medicine*, 1997, 25 pp. 22–4.

Appendix 3

1. Baker et al., 'Concussion among under-20 rugby union players in Ireland'.

2. Bird et al., 'The New Zealand rugby injury and performance project'.

3. Collins et al., 'Injuries sustained by high school rugby players in the United States, 2005–2006'.

4. Cusimano et al., 'Mechanisms of team-sport-related brain injuries in children 5 to 19 years old'.

5. Davidson et al., 'Casualty room presentations and schoolboy rugby union'.

6. Davidson, 'Schoolboy rugby injuries, 1969–1986'.

7. Durie et al., 'A prospective survey of injuries in a New Zealand schoolboy rugby population'.

8. Finch et al., 'Sport and active recreation injuries in Australia'.

9. Fuller et al., 'Epidemiological study of injuries in men's international under-20 rugby union tournaments'.

10. T. J. Gabbett, 'Performance changes following a field conditioning program in junior and senior rugby league players', *Journal of Strength and Conditioning Research*, National Strength and Conditioning Association, 2006, 20(1) pp. 215–21.

11. Gabbett, 'Incidence of injury in junior rugby league players over four competitive seasons'.

12. Garraway et al., 'Impact of professionalism'.

13. Haseler et al., 'The epidemiology of injuries in English youth community rugby union'.

14. Junge et al., 'Injuries in youth amateur soccer and rugby players'.

15. Lee, 'Epidemiological comparison of injuries in school and senior club rugby'.

16. Lewis et al., 'An initial investigation of injuries in women, men and youths playing Rugby Union football at the same club'.

17. MacLean et al., 'Serious neck injuries in U19 rugby union players'.

18. Marshall et al., 'Concussion in rugby: the hidden epidemic'.

19. McIntosh et al., 'Head, face and neck injury in youth rugby'.

20. McManus et al., 'Incidence of injury in elite junior Rugby Union'.

21. Nathan et al., 'The incidence and nature of rugby injuries'.

22. Nicol et al., 'Rugby union injuries in Scottish schools'.

23. Palmer-Green et al., 'Match injuries in English youth academy and schools rugby union'.

24. Pringle, 'Incidence of sporting injury in New Zealand youths aged 6–15 years'.

25. Roux et al., 'The epidemiology of schoolboy rugby injuries'.
26. Shuttleworth-Edwards et al., 'The comparative incidence of reported concussions presenting for follow-up management in South African Rugby Union'.
27. Sparks, 'Half a million hours of rugby football'.
28. Sparks, 'Rugby football injuries, 1980–1983'.
29. Sparks, 'Half a million hours of rugby football'.
30. Sugerman, 'Injuries in an Australian schools rugby union season'.
31. Upton et al., 'Inadequate pre-season preparation of schoolboy rugby players'.
32. Usman et al., 'Upper limb injury in rugby union football'.
33. M. A. Weir, A. W. Watson, 'A twelve month study of sports injuries in one Irish school', *Irish Journal of Medical Science*, 1996, 165(3) pp. 165–9.

Appendix 4

1. Gabbett, 'Performance changes following a field conditioning program in junior and senior rugby league players'.
2. Junge et al., 'Injuries in youth amateur soccer and rugby players'.
3. Nathan et al., 'The incidence and nature of rugby injuries'.
4. Roux et al., 'The epidemiology of schoolboy rugby injuries'.
5. Sparks, 'Rugby football injuries, 1980–1983'.
6. Bird et al., 'The New Zealand Rugby Injury and Performance Project'.
7. Collins et al., 'Injuries sustained by high school rugby players in the United States, 2005–2006'.
8. Marshall et al., 'Concussion in rugby: the hidden epidemic'.

Further Reading

1. Stephen Wagg, Carlton Brick, Belinda Wheaton, Jayne Caudwell. *Key Concepts in Sports Studies*. SAGE, 2009.
2. Paolo David. *Human Rights in Youth Sport: A Critical Review of Children's Rights in Competitive Sport*. Routledge, 2004.
3. Fred Coalter. *A Wider Social Role for Sport: Who's Keeping the Score?* Routledge, 2007.

The author's website is www.allysonpollock.com

Index